MindShifts

D1717157

MindShifts

A Brain-Based Process for Restructuring Schools and Renewing Education

Geoffrey Caine
Renate Nummela Caine
Sam Crowell

Zephyr
Press

Tucson, Arizona

MindShifts
A Brain-Based Process for Restructuring Schools and Renewing Education

Grades: All ages

Printed in the United States of America

ISBN 1-56976-007-1

Editors: Stacey Lynn and Stacey Shropshire
Cover design: David Fischer
Design and production: Nancy Taylor
Typesetting: Casa Cold Type, Inc.
Photographs: Debbie Crowell

Zephyr Press
P.O. Box 66006
Tucson, Arizona 85728-6006

Library of Congress Cataloging-in-Publication Data

Caine, Geoffrey.
    MindShifts : a brain-based process for restructuring schools and
renewing education / Geoffrey Caine, Renate Nummela Caine, Sam
Crowell.
        p. cm.
    Includes bibliographical references and index.
    ISBN 1-56976-007-1
    1. Learning, Psychology of. 2. Teaching. 3. Educational change.
4. Brain. I. Caine, Renate Nummela. II. Crowell, Sam.
III. Title: Mindshifts
LB1060.C33 1994
370.15'23—dc20   94-27925

What are the sources of order?
How do we create organizational coherence,
where activities correspond to purpose?
How do we create structures that move with change,
that are flexible and adaptive, even boundaryless,
that enable rather than constrain?
How do we simplify things without losing both
control and differentiation? How do we resolve personal
needs for freedom and autonomy with organizational
needs for prediction and control?

— Margaret J. Wheatley

As Einstein is often quoted as saying:
No problem can be solved from the same consciousness
that created it. We must learn to see the world anew.

— Margaret J. Wheatley

Contents

Contents

Part III
Making It Happen

Appendixes

Preface

Once upon a time, on a planet much like ours, there were lots of people who had to make long and hazardous journeys to get where they were going from where they were. An elite group of tour guides was responsible for leading them. The journeys were often a thousand miles and more, over mountains, across deserts, through swamps. Hostile bands had to be avoided or defeated without anyone's being injured. The guides had to provide food, water, and shelter. Yet more and more people wanted to travel, and they all demanded to arrive in good condition and on time.

The tour guides were fed up. They were overworked, underpaid, highly stressed, and . . . rather annoyed.

During one of their rare breaks, when conditions were even worse than usual, and during a moment of even more uncommon silence, one of their number was heard to say: "I had a strange dream last night. I dreamed that we crossed the mountains and the deserts faster than a speeding bullet, and we had so much free time left that we got to go to planet Earth for a holiday."

So frustrated were her colleagues that they did not dismiss the dream out of hand. Instead there was a question: "How did you do it?"

Silence, then an answer. "We could fly."

As educators we cannot deal in the old way with the mountains and deserts and hostile forces anymore. There are just too many. We have no alternative. We have to learn how to fly. In practical terms, this means that we have to deal with education differently from the ways in which we have dealt with it in the past.

We must come to a new and different understanding of what we actually have to do, so that we can see how to get beyond teaching by crisis management. It is not just a matter of finding new things to do. It is a matter of profoundly reconceptualizing what it is that we are trying to accomplish.

This workbook is written for educators who are interested in meaningful learning. It is not just a recipe book with techniques to boost memorization, though memory in fact does increase dramatically when learning is meaningful. Nor is it a "how-to" book with techniques that work wonders for educators who do not understand what they are doing.

MindShifts is designed to increase your awareness of how the brain learns and to provide you with tools and procedures that enable you to design your own techniques and effective learning environments. It is based on the assumption that meaningful learning is developmental and leads to genuine personal change, and that school restructuring is developmental and leads to genuine systemic change.

Because all effective learning involves some uncertainty and confusion, we have not written in the hope that everything will make complete sense after the first reading. You should not expect or seek mastery of any section before you explore another section. Each section of the book is designed to throw light on every other section. Therefore, you can proceed through the workbook systematically or dip into sections in any order you prefer. You may even find yourself reworking some sections several times.

Every student and every teacher has immeasurable untapped reserves of competence and creativity. As you better appreciate how your brain learns, how it creates and processes information, you will begin to access more of those hidden reserves, as will your students. Then you can better meet the challenge and experience the fulfillment to which you as an educator are entitled.

Story Line

We begin with an introduction in which we spell out the basic assumptions that have guided us, and we provide an overview of how to make best use of this book.

In part one, we introduce a distinction between a theory and a mental model. We also explain the importance of dealing with individual growth and systemic change simultaneously.

We include some exercises that enable you to assess your current mental model of how people learn and schools work. We introduce a way to reconceptualize outcomes. We conclude by setting up a study-group process.

Part two is an in-depth exploration of the twelve principles of brain functioning. We have included group activities, questions to ask yourself about teaching and learning, and organizational principles that begin to tie instruction, curriculum, and organization together. This section culminates with a review of the model of brain-based instruction and the roles that teachers and non-teachers play.

In part three, we spell out the overall theory upon which brain-based instruction is founded. Here we provide a larger framework for connecting and integrating the host of strategies and materials that are now available.

Finally, there are appendixes in which we supply additional exercises and processes, including a description of four perceptual styles, which will help you in working with children and with each other.

This book was designed to assist you in establishing a flexible and powerful foundation for your learning community. You will begin to appreciate the underlying and often invisible patterns around which education forms. And you will set in motion the new patterns that must guide you on the journey upon which you are embarking.

Introduction

Using This Book

What This Book Is About

This is a book about changing teaching and about changing schools. It deals with the two processes simultaneously because each influences the other and because *they are both aspects of the same general process.* Therefore, as we come to understand one better, we will also understand the other.

Students who learn well are those who can handle a significant amount of confusion and "active uncertainty." This ability to handle uncertainty is absolutely crucial because the students' ideas are being reorganized and there must be a time of transition between what students already know and what they come to know as they learn.

The same is true of a school that changes. It must be able to deal with a significant amount of turbulence because there must be a time of transition from a stable system (what it has been in the past) to a reorganized system (what it will become). A mind that is in the midst of some confusion is like a system that is in the midst of some turbulence and chaos.

Fortunately, both learning and change can be facilitated. What matters most in both cases is the basic set of ideas that we use to guide us in what we do.

Guiding Assumptions

In this book we make a number of assumptions about learning and change. Following we list these assumptions and the actions that this book facilitates in regard to each assumption.

1. The way in which we teach depends upon our mental model of how people learn.

Peter Senge (1990) notes, "'Mental Models' are deeply ingrained assumptions, generalizations, or even pictures or images that influence how we understand the world and how we take actions. Very often, we are not consciously aware of our mental models or the effects they have on our behavior" (8). Senge notes further that there is often a difference between our "espoused theories" (what we say) and what Chris Argyris calls our "theories in use"—our mental models. According to Argyris, we do not always behave congruently with what we say, but we do act congruently with what we believe (Senge 1990, 175).

Why do we have grades? Why are subjects either kept separate or integrated? What is the function of pull-out programs? What role do teachers and support staff play in administration? What is the place for whole language, whole math, and whole science? Should the arts and sciences be integrated? What connections should there be between the classroom and the wider community?

There is often a difference between how we answer these questions out loud and the actions that we take. It is what we actually believe—our mental model—that drives every decision we make and every strategy we select. The first key to improving learning, therefore, is for everyone involved in education to have a powerful and accurate mental model of how people learn.

ACTION

Use this book as a process book to assist you in creating a new mental model of learning.

---

2. That mental model should be based on the best research we have about how the brain actually learns.

We are all designed for learning. It is as natural as breathing. And just as our lungs and respiratory systems have been designed for their functions, so the brain is designed for learning. Fortunately, researchers now know a lot about how the brain does its job. Renate and Geoffrey Caine (1994) translated research into a set of principles and a theory of great practical value for educators. We need to understand and internalize, as a mental model that guides us, the theory of brain-based learning and teaching.

ACTION

Use part 2 of the book, which contains a set of activities and explanations about each of the brain principles, to help you understand those principles in depth.

---

3. One of the best ways to enhance or acquire a new mental model is to examine our own learning and experience.

The way in which experts learn always involves reflection upon their own experience. That principle of learning also emerges out of brain research. In fact, it is quite extraordinary that some of the processes we have all used and have become competent in—as we mastered a hobby, for instance—often get left at the door to the classroom.

We are all professionals, those of us in the classroom and those of us in other roles. As professionals, we need to spend an appropriate amount of time examining our own practices and our own past best performances and less-than-best performances. That is the raw material out of which further expertise emerges.

Unfortunately, educators and support staff usually do not have time to reflect upon what they have done and what they have learned. Most reflection is limited to thinking about what has to be done next. Hence we must establish a process, supported by the educational system, that generates and sustains the type of reflection that we need.

ACTION

Set up study groups supported by the system in which honest, creative, and effective reflection and sharing are possible.

You may be able to set up groups that meet during school time. Where there is no group, carry out the reflection with a colleague or individually. You will have opportunities to reflect on what did and did not work for you as a child and in other contexts. In time, your reflection will begin to shift toward teachers and administrators becoming ongoing researchers into their own professional activities.

4. **For a school to change, almost all adults must share the same mental model of learning so that all their decisions and interactions are mutually reinforcing.**

Perhaps the most important idea to grasp is that change and growth must occur in both individual and collective ways. On the one hand, we are all unique, with beliefs and values and experiences and preferences and our own personal styles. On the other hand, we are all simultaneously members of small and large groups that we influence and that influence what we do.

Each one of us is called upon to make countless decisions that have an impact on the school as a whole. There is no way that we can collaborate on everything. It is the totality of our taken-for-granted agreements and underlying beliefs and purposes that will help or hinder systemic change. When we base our individual decisions on the same underlying ideas, in almost every case the system as a whole will be in our minds as well, and the system as a whole will be improved.

ACTION

Use the study process to investigate the principles of brain functioning.

As you investigate, you will learn from each other, develop your own points of view, and also develop a common perspective—a shared mental model based upon brain research—about teaching, learning, and support.

5. **The basis for effective long-term change is the creation of a healthy and supportive learning community in the school as a whole that makes it possible for the new mental model to be implemented.**

One of the principles that emerges from research is that learning is inhibited by threat and enhanced by challenge. This principle does not mean that we should never feel anxious, but it is difficult to learn when we feel helpless or fatigued. The principle applies just as much to us as to our students.

The emerging consensus is that our first task is to create supportive and healthy learning communities. As Joyce and others say in *The Self-Renewing School,* "All personnel become students of school improvement. An integrated culture of professionals is developed." A self-renewing school is a place where all participants are learning, where learning itself is valued, where there is a sense of comradery and cooperation, where there is adherence to at least some common values and procedures, and where there is an underlying sense of orderliness and commitment to a common purpose.

ACTION

Use the communication procedures in this workbook to develop a shared sense of orderliness and safety that infuses the school as a whole.

The result will be an emergent atmosphere of mutual respect and support for individual growth and school change.

Until one is committed, there is hesitancy, the chance to draw back, always ineffectiveness, concerning all acts of initiative (and creation). There is one elementary truth the ignorance of which kills countless ideas and splendid plans: that the moment one definitely commits oneself, then Providence moves too. All sorts of things occur to help one that would never otherwise have occurred. A whole stream of events issues from the decision, raising in one's favor all manner of unforeseen incidents and meetings and material assistance which no man could have dreamed would have come his way. Whatever you can do or dream you can, begin it. Boldness has genius, power, and magic in it. **Begin it now.**

— Johann Wolfgang von Goethe

This Is a Process Book

Difficulties are opportunities to better things;
they are stepping stones to greater experience.

— Brian Adams

The implication of lifelong learning is that there is no one outcome. We are on a journey, and the key is to appreciate each step—to enjoy the journey and to learn as we go.

We all want to be better educators, functioning in more exciting and effective educational environments. There are also some indicators of how successful we have become. However, simply setting our sights on a goal will never lead us to the goal we actually seek. In part that is because *to the extent that we are operating from old mental models we are not capable of knowing exactly what a much better system will look like.*

Because we cannot know what a better system looks like, we must combine the setting of goals with remaining open to what emerges, which is a major change in our mental model of how things work. Neither people nor schools are machines. Both the human mind and the learning organization are more like collections of flowing rivers. Real learning is ongoing. And in a complex world, the systems that survive and flourish must be dynamic and capable of constant change.

Our approach has been to search for a process that constantly generates insights and flexible adaptation while developing stability and security. The journey is never clear sailing. We must move through inertia to get started; there are occasional uncertainties and doubts but also the sense of joy and comfort as we connect with each other; there is the reluctance to make further changes as well as the excitement of constant breakthroughs; and the list goes on.

Change, of course, takes time. All learning is developmental, including the learning of educators. Many of the changes that are needed will also appear in unexpected ways and from unpredictable sources. Some of the most unlikely people will become the most valuable colleagues and collaborators. The change from fragmentation to a higher degree of order is not easy. It is clear, however, that when the right conditions are established, the transition can occur. Setting out to participate in the change is exciting, challenging and immensely rewarding.

— Caine 1994, 194

Hints and Ideas for Using This Book

Here are some recommendations to assist you in gaining the maximum value for your time and effort. You will find that they help you to implement and experience directly many of the ideas that we discuss in more depth later on in this workbook and in the ones to follow.

- **Read *Making Connections: Teaching and the Human Brain*.**
  Although *MindShifts* is self-contained, it is based on *Making Connections*. Read *Making Connections* once, then refer back to it as you explore the contents of this book. That intensive exploration is essential to grasping the content at the depth required for major transformation.

- **Take your time**.
  Ongoing consistency of effort is much more valuable than one brief, intensive examination of the contents. There is a rhythm to learning, in part because meaningful learning engages the entire body, brain, and mind. As you sense those rhythms yourself, you will become better equipped to invoke them in your students.

- **Keep a journal**.
  Our experience supports the power of journal writing as a vehicle for self-teaching. You will have invaluable insights of your own as you deal with our materials. Such insights may be lost if they are not recorded. In fact, keeping a journal actually helps you to reflect and to have the insights that you need. It is one aspect of the active processing of experience that we deal with in depth in other places. We have left spaces throughout the book for you to record your thoughts, notes, drawings, doodles, and mind maps, but keeping a journal will increase the benefit you derive from using this book.

- **Have a project or relevant and personal application in mind**.
  We suggest that you examine these materials with a specific goal or project in mind. That could be anything from the way you teach a specific subject to a matter of social concern over which you wish to have some influence. This project will significantly enhance your own learning.

- **Use the techniques in appendix B and elsewhere frequently, but do NOT decide in advance how they are going to work or what the effects will be**.
  You will see that the final section of this workbook consists of techniques and procedures. We refer to them at various points in other sections where their use is encouraged. However, our goal is more than skill development or "getting it right." Our techniques are designed to generate experiences that help to provide an overall and deeper sense of how people experience meaning and acquire natural knowledge or understanding. The techniques are to be explored in contexts that seem appropriate to you and not simply practiced on someone.

- **Cultivate and welcome active uncertainty as a state of mind**.
  Genuine learning involves genuinely changing our minds. Although we need to relate what we study to what we know, we cannot afford to reduce what we study to what we currently believe and understand. The in-between state, which may involve a sense of confusion and incompleteness, is absolutely vital in our students and therefore we must accept and understand it.

- **Set up a study group to work through the ideas and activities**.
  We have developed a set of guidelines for groups to follow, and we spell them out in depth in chapter 5.

However, there are may ways to set up groups—both within a school and beyond the boundaries of a school. The bottom line is that these are groups for reflecting in an honest and orderly way upon your personal experiences. They are not problem-solving groups; they do not have a prescribed administrative agenda; and they are not to be controlled by outsiders telling the members what to do.

As the concepts and procedures in this book become a part of your natural knowledge, you will change and how you view teaching will change. Such changes may include

your sense of time

your definition of learning

your assessment of outcomes

your view of the school as an educating community

and more.

Begin slowly and gently and build success in your own way and in your own world before you seek to change other teachers, parents, or administrators. We all need to go through the process itself.

Encourage rather than criticize.

Demonstrate rather than tell.

PART I
Setting the Stage

Story

Somewhere in a galaxy not far away a story is being told. It doesn't have a name yet. That is why it is referred to as Story. But it knows that much of what has been taught about learning and teaching is wrong. And that is why it is on a quest.

It knows (and has known for a long time) that there are beings in the universe who can hear it—sometimes faintly and sometimes clear as a bell.

Once it popped into the head of a football coach when his team was right on the opponent's goal line. He didn't pay attention . . . and Story didn't get through.

A few thousand years ago a baby was with its mother by the side of a great river. It heard Story. Trouble was, the baby couldn't speak yet and Story got lost.

But it persisted!

It kept on circling the Earth and popping into the noosphere. Every few years it found more and more people who were curious, who heard fragments and wanted more. Those people began to meet each other and share thoughts, and they found that each of them had a different part of Story. And to their surprise, as they delved deeper and deeper into the parts they understood, they found Story there in its entirety, waiting . . .

Learn to unclutter your mind.
Learn to simplify your work.

— John Heider, *The Tao of Leadership*

1

Exploring Mental Models

The Real Problem

The biggest problem facing educators is that there are too many problems. For example, we have to prepare students to pass tests devised by others, on content selected by others. Our classes are full of people from a variety of cultural backgrounds, often speaking languages that we do not know.

Students come from backgrounds that may be deprived or enriched, secure or threatening, healthy or drug afflicted. We work with more people than can be managed, with inadequate resources and in content areas that often are not our fields of expertise. And all this occurs within a system of administration that often seems to be indifferent to the needs of the people in it.

Add to this all the strategies and practices that are currently being advocated.

To how many of the following issues are you being exposed?

Authentic experience	Block scheduling
Authentic assessment	Site-based management
Whole language	Cross-age and peer tutoring
Reading recovery	Constructivism
Thematic instruction	Full inclusion
Technological innovations	Multiculturalism
Integrated curriculum	Limited English proficiency
Cooperative learning	New state-mandated curricula

List some of the other issues that are arising or strategies and processes that are being introduced in some way into your professional environment.

The situation often looks and feels hopeless. To what extent is this true for you?

The point to understand is that the way we have been addressing the situation does leave us hopeless. We simply cannot succeed by doing things the way they have always been done. That brings us back to our initial point. We have too many problems, and it is not possible to solve them all—one at a time.

We have been dealing with issues one at a time. We have been given a host of specific solutions for specific problems, which has happened because our dominant mental model in education has been to see everything as mechanical. The machine metaphor leads us to believe that each part can be disassembled and treated separately, but that is no longer possible.

Our challenge is to realize that all our problems are somehow related. They are connected to each other and they cause each other. We will finally turn education around, in our classrooms and in our communities, when we adequately grasp the nature of that connectedness. Then we will also see how to deal with our problems simultaneously.

The way to begin is to examine the situation as it is. First, we need to take stock of some of our current basic beliefs and examine our current mental model. Second, we need to assess the climate and nature of our current school community. We will then be in a position to develop a more powerful mental model and to set in motion a process for generating the sort of learning community that nurtures and supports significant change.

What Is a Mental Model?

A mental model is a personal, deeply held belief that drives what we do and how we do it. Mental models are beliefs about ourselves, others, what works and what doesn't, and how things happen. These models do not necessarily have anything to do with a formal theory or what we learned in school. Those theories tend to be associated with formal knowledge, which may or may not actually influence what happens in our classrooms. We tend to act on the basis of our much more personal, deeply held mental models.

Whenever we do anything, be it asking questions, answering questions, giving advice, or designing a lesson, a personal theory drives us. For example, a mental model might hold that children are blank slates waiting to absorb new knowledge provided by the teacher. A teacher whose mental model reflects this kind of belief will think and behave differently from one with a mental model that holds that children are active meaning makers born to make sense of their world and participate in their own learning. Let us imagine some consequences deriving from these two mental models.

Notes

Notes

Possible thoughts of a teacher who believes that children are blank slates:

- I must present the material correctly.

- I can tell when my students have learned because they know the right answers.

- The more information the child can absorb, the better teacher I am.

Possible thoughts of a teacher who believes that students are active meaning makers:

- I have to create learning experiences that allow children of many styles and ability levels to benefit.

- As much as possible, the children need to be challenged to ask their own questions and research the possible answers.

- I can tell that my students have learned when they can actively describe what they know to others. They can demonstrate, perform, or exhibit a product for assessment by a wide variety of peers, adults, and experts.

Most mental models are a mixture of beliefs. The most critical thing to remember about them is that mental models may have little to do with the formal explanations we give to others. Therefore, some teachers would automatically say that they believe all children can learn (formal explanation), but if we observe what they do in the classroom, their actions and decisions are not congruent with their articulated beliefs.

Most teachers are not aware of the mental models that drive them. Because we have not examined our mental models openly (have not actively processed them), they continue to govern our thoughts and decisions.

Changing mental models is not easy because it is difficult to see clearly, and thus have the potential to change, our deepest assumptions. Any genuine attempt to shift a mental model (resulting in different behaviors) is frequently met with some feelings of uncertainty.

Here is an example of how mental models in mathematics determine how we teach.

Mike Fellows is a research mathematician who believes that the same questions that confound research professors at the graduate university level are appropriate dilemmas for elementary school children to study. Many of his colleagues would argue with him. How would you react? What are your present mental models that might prevent you from accepting this idea?

(Be honest with yourself—this is not a test.) Would you like to hear more?

Mike feels that the questions that confound computer analysts and designers of artificial intelligence form the basis of broader questions linking mathematics to real life. One example he uses relates to the question of "sorting." Sorting, simply put, focuses on the smallest number of connections necessary to create a complex system. To translate this concept into a problem for third graders, we must create efficient models. Examples include designing paved streets for a community that has limited funds and in which every house must be connected by pavement at the lowest expense possible.

Unpacking Fundamental Concepts

It is useful to "unpack" the central concepts that guide education and see what deeper meanings they have for us. In fact, one indicator of change and growth is our deepening appreciation of the meaning and implication of those fundamental concepts. As "learning," "teaching," and "schooling" are among the central ideas that need to be reconceptualized, we will begin with them. We are asking you to think about what the terms mean. Whether you have or have not thought about these ideas recently, you need to arrive at a realistic and personal definition.

One useful technique to use is webbing.

Step 1 Simply place the basic idea in the center of your page (or begin by experimenting with the space on these two pages), then allow as many associations to come to mind as you can.

Step 2 Write down your thoughts anywhere on the page.

Step 3 After you have brainstormed in this way, see if there is a basic general pattern or idea that explains your central understanding of the concept.

Step 4 Write half a page to a page about what you really think the concept means. (You might also like to note the date on which these answers came to mind.)

What does *learning* mean to you?

What is teaching?

Where is school?

What is the core curriculum?

What is the best way to find out what children have learned?

Who are a child's most influential teachers?

What other key concepts or constructs would you like to explore?

Further Exploration: Testing Assumptions

Sometimes we find that our practice reflects assumptions that we do not really have. This happened recently to one of us.

> *Sam was teaching a class based on the creative development of new teachers in the classroom. He noticed that there seemed to be unnecessary anxiety concerning one of the assignments he gave to the class. The students were focused on getting the procedures exactly right, whereas what Sam wanted was for the students to access their creativity.*
>
> *He realized that there was a hidden assumption in the way the course was communicated and the way the assignment was designed. Students wanted to "do well." To them, "doing well" meant the assignment had to be done in a certain way. Sam did not agree with that assumption nor had he ever stated it. In fact, he took pains to lessen students' anxiety. But there it was.*

We have identified a number of rather mechanistic assumptions that are suggested by a great deal of our practice in schools. These are not necessarily things that educators "believe"; rather they are beliefs that our practices "suggest" we believe. What is interesting is how quickly and firmly students pick up on unstated assumptions. This is even more true when these unstated assumptions pervade the very essence of the educational process, school itself.

None of these assumptions is supported by research about the way the brain engages in meaningful learning. Yet educational practice based on these assumptions contributes to a lack of meaning in learning and teaching.

How many of these are held by you or are reflected in the practices in your school?

- We can control and largely manipulate outcomes.
- Testing is generally a good motivator for meaningful learning.

Notes

- Positive reinforcement controlled by others is a proven way to help children learn anything important.

- Subjects are best learned when separated and taught within discrete time periods.

- Memorization for tests is the most effective way for students to learn.

- The arts are for artists and have nothing to do with cognition.

- Physical movement is unrelated to learning.

- We can force students to engage in meaningful learning by threatening to punish them for misbehavior and poor performance or by spelling out a direct reward ahead of time.

- Learning has to be done individually and alone.

- There is only one correct answer and there is only one way to arrive at that answer.

- There is a straight cause-effect relationship between teacher contact and student learning.

- The sequence in which knowledge is to be acquired has a fixed and best order.

- By acquiring a set of incremental skills, students will suddenly know how to read or to perform in complex ways.

- If students do not learn what we want them to learn, then something is wrong with the students.

- Acquiring concepts is a strictly cognitive process unrelated to attitude and unshaped by emotion.

- Learning is primarily reflected in behavioral changes observable by us in our classrooms.

- Students learn only when "paying attention."

- Schools are the only or the primary places of learning.

- Memory always requires memorization.

- We can control and separate learning from social interaction.

- Once students have memorized the "rules" they will not misbehave.

Questions to begin to ask yourself:

What kind of learning happens without direct instruction?

What are some of the things students "learn" instantly?

What forms of assessment challenge learners without triggering a sense of helplessness in them?

What would be different in your school if everyone believed that:

    All subjects could and should be combined and interconnected?

    Learning occurs over time—sometimes slowly and sometimes quickly?

    The real indicators of meaningful learning are often not apparent on a test?

    Emotions actually influence understanding?

Understanding does not come from adding up incremental bits and pieces of knowledge but from engaging in projects and processes that generate a sense of completion from the very beginning?

Teachers are not always right?

Your comments

How Do We Begin the Change?

One way to change how education is practiced is to change the ideas we hold about it. Once we are no longer bound by entrenched assumptions that permeate much of education, we are free to develop new ideas. This book is intended to open up possibilities. As we begin to realize that teaching can be an art of its own and that learning involves a vast array of complex experiences, a whole new excitement takes place. We have the freedom to BE educators.

This book is not a set of unworkable ideas. In fact, many educators already have an understanding of these concepts. Yet in some cases they are not a part of our conscious perceptions or are beyond our ability to articulate clearly. Significantly, the principles and ideas this book introduces are based upon the latest research available on how the human brain processes learning.

We have purposely not tried to make this a scientific explanation. Rather, we have developed activities to help you experience what these principles feel like when they are put into practice. Once we have a feel for something it is easier to generate our own ideas and unique expressions. For the artist, technique is developed to help accomplish an idea, not as an end in itself. The applications of these ideas are limitless.

We call this book *MindShifts* because the principles about the ways we learn contradict many of the under-lying assumptions practiced in our schools today. Accepting these ideas requires us to begin shifting our thinking to new assumptions.

Let's face it; we all know that changes in education need to take place. Many of the changes are social, political, and economic in nature. Others are organizational and structural. Still others involve ways in which we directly interact with students in places we call classrooms.

We invite you to test, examine, and explore the brain principles that follow. As you grasp the richness and complexity of the operations carried on in every learning brain, you will be in a better position to make the changes needed to teach for meaning.

We underrate our brain and our intelligence. . . .
[R]eluctance to learn cannot be attributed to the
brain. Learning is the brain's primary function, its
constant concern, and we become restless and
frustrated if there is no learning to be done. We are
all capable of huge and unsuspected learning
accomplishments without effort.

— Frank Smith, *Insult to Intelligence*

2

Principles of Brain-Based Learning*

Our objective is to summarize the accumulated insights of the research in a form that is of practical benefit to educators. The summary and consolidation take the form of twelve principles that can serve as a general theoretical foundation for brain-based learning.

These principles provide us with a framework for learning and teaching that moves us irrevocably away from the methods and models that have dominated education for more than a century. The behavioral model, particularly as practiced in education, must be put to rest. What replaces it is an open quest bound primarily by the limitations we choose and place on ourselves and the dictates of the human brain itself. If we become overwhelmed by the lack of the right answer or procedure as we let go of certainty, we can perhaps seek comfort in the thought that above all else, brain-based learning opens doors. It is time that we moved on.

1. **The brain is a parallel processor.**
    It is always doing many things at one time (Ornstein and Sobel 1987). Thoughts, emotions, imagination, and predispositions operate simultaneously and interact with other modes of information processing and the expansion of general social and cultural knowledge.

---

*This chapter is a modified version of chapter 7 in *Making Connections: Teaching and the Human Brain.*

Implications for education: Good teaching "orchestrates" the learner's experience so that all these aspects of brain operation are addressed. Teaching must, therefore, be based on theories and methodologies that guide the teacher so as to make orchestration possible. No one method or technique can by itself adequately encompass the variations of the human brain. However, teachers do need a frame of reference that enables them to select from the vast repertoire of methods and approaches that are available.

2. **Learning engages the entire physiology.**
The brain is a physiological organ functioning according to physiological rules. Learning is as natural as breathing, but it can be inhibited or facilitated. Neuron growth, nourishment, and interactions are integral to the perception and interpretation of experiences (Diamond 1985). Stress and threat affect the brain differently than do peace, challenge, boredom, happiness, and contentment (Ornstein and Sobel 1987). In fact some aspects of the actual "wiring" of the brain are affected by school and life experiences.

Implications for education: Everything that affects our physiological functioning affects our capacity to learn. Stress management, nutrition, exercise, and relaxation, as well as other facets of health management, must be fully incorporated into the learning process. As many drugs, both prescribed and recreational, inhibit learning, their use should be curtailed and their effects understood. Habits and beliefs are also physiologically entrenched and therefore resistant or slow to change once they become part of the personality. In addition, the timing of learning is influenced by the body's and brain's natural development as well as by individual and natural rhythms and cycles. For example, there can be a five-year difference in maturation between any two "average" children. Expecting achievement on the basis of chronological age is therefore inappropriate.

3. **The search for meaning (making sense of our experiences) and the consequential need to act on our environment is automatic.**
   The search for meaning is survival oriented and basic to the human brain. The brain needs and automatically registers the familiar while simultaneously searching for and responding to novel stimuli (O'Keefe and Nadel 1978). This dual process is taking place every waking moment and, some contend, while sleeping. Other research confirms the notion that people are meaning makers (see chapter 8 of *Making Connections*). The search for meaning cannot be stopped, only channeled and focused.

   Implications for education: The learning environment needs to provide stability and familiarity, which is part of the function of routine classroom behaviors and procedures. At the same time, provision must be made to satisfy our curiosity and hunger for novelty, discovery, and challenge. Lessons need to be generally exciting and meaningful and offer students an abundance of choices. The more positively like real life such learning is, the better. Programs for gifted children often take these implications for granted by combining a rich environment with complex and meaningful challenges. In our view most of the creative methods used for teaching gifted students should be applied to all students.

4. **The search for meaning takes place by "patterning."** (Nummela and Rosengren 1986). Patterning refers to the meaningful organization and categorization of information. In a way, the brain is both artist and scientist, attempting to discern and understand patterns as they occur, and giving expression to unique and creative patterns of its own. The brain is designed to perceive and generate patterns, and it resists having meaningless patterns imposed on it. By "meaningless" we mean isolated pieces of information unrelated to what makes sense to a student. When the brain's natural capacity to

integrate information is acknowledged and invoked in teaching, then vast amounts of initially unrelated or seemingly random information and activities can be presented and assimilated.

Implications for education: Learners are patterning, or perceiving and creating meanings, all the time in one way or another. We cannot stop them; we can only influence the direction. Daydreaming is a way of patterning, as are problem solving and critical thinking. Although we choose much of what students are to learn, the ideal process is to present the information in a way that allows their brains to extract patterns, rather than attempt to impose the patterns. "Time on task" does not ensure appropriate patterning, because the student may actually be engaged in busy work while the mind is somewhere else. For teaching to be really effective, a learner must be able to create meaningful and personally relevant patterns. This type of teaching is supported by those advocating a whole language approach to reading (Goodman 1986; Altweger, Edelsky, and Flores 1987), thematic teaching (Kovalik 1989), integration of the curriculum (Shalley 1988), and approaches to learning that are relevant to life outside the classroom.

5. **Emotions are critical and at the heart of patterning.**
We do not simply learn things. What we learn is influenced and organized by emotions and mind-sets based on expectancy, personal biases and prejudices, degree of self-esteem, and the need for social interaction. Emotions and cognition cannot be separated (Ornstein and Sobel 1987; Lakoff 1987; McGuinness and Pribram 1980; and Halgren and others 1983). Emotions are also crucial to memory because they facilitate the storage and recall of information (Rosenfield 1988). Moreover, many emotions cannot be simply switched on and off. They operate on many levels, somewhat like the weather, and they are

ongoing—the emotional impact of any lesson or life experience may continue to reverberate long after the specific event.

Implications for education: Teachers need to understand that students' feelings and attitudes will be involved in and will determine future learning. As it is impossible to isolate the cognitive from the affective domain, the emotional climate in the school and classroom must be monitored on a consistent basis, by using effective communication strategies and allowing for student and teacher reflection and metacognitive processes. In general, the entire environment needs to be supportive and marked by mutual respect and acceptance both within and beyond the classroom. Some of the most significant experiences in a student's life are fleeting "moments of truth," such as a chance encounter in a corridor with a relatively unknown teacher or possibly "distant" administrator. These brief communications are often instinctive. Their emotional color depends on how "real" and profound the support for each other of teachers, administrators, and students is.

6. **The brain processes parts and wholes simultaneously.**
    There is evidence of brain laterality, meaning that there are significant differences between left and right hemispheres of the brain (Springer and Deutsch 1985). However, in a healthy person the two hemispheres are inextricably interactive, irrespective of whether a person is dealing with words, mathematics, music, or art (Hand 1984; Hart 1975; Levy 1972). The "two brain" doctrine is most valuable as a metaphor that assists educators to acknowledge two separate but simultaneous tendencies in the brain for organizing information. One is to reduce such information into parts; the other is to perceive and work with information as a whole or a series of wholes.

Notes

Implications for education: People have enormous difficulty in learning when either parts or wholes are overlooked. Good teaching necessarily builds understanding and skills over time because learning is cumulative and developmental. However, parts and wholes are conceptually interactive. They derive meaning from and give it to each other. Thus vocabulary and grammar are best understood and mastered when incorporated in genuine, whole language experiences. Similarly, equations and scientific principles need to be dealt with in the context of living science.

7. **Learning involves both focused attention and peripheral perception.**
   The brain absorbs information of which it is directly aware and to which it is paying attention. It also directly absorbs information and signals that lie beyond the field of attention. Such signals may be stimuli that one perceives "out of the side of the eyes" such as grey and unattractive walls in a classroom. Peripheral stimuli also include the very "light" or subtle signals that are within the field of attention but are still not consciously noticed (such as a hint of a smile or slight changes in body posture). The brain responds to the entire sensory context in which teaching or communication occurs (O'Keefe and Nadel 1978).

   One of Lozanov's (1978) fundamental principles is that every stimulus is coded, associated, and symbolized. Thus, every sound, from a word to a siren, and every visual signal, from a blank screen to a raised finger, is packed full of complex meanings. For example, a simple knock on the door engages attention and is processed for possible meaning by reference both to much of a learner's prior knowledge and experience and to whatever is happening at the moment. Peripheral information can therefore be purposely "organized" to facilitate learning.

Implications for education: The teacher can and should organize materials that will be outside of the focus of the learner's attention. In addition to noise, temperature, and so on, peripherals include visuals such as charts, illustrations, set designs, and art, including great works of art. Barzakov (1988) recommends that art be changed frequently to reflect changes in learning focus. Educators have also begun to recognize the use of music as a way to enhance and influence more natural acquisition of information.

The subtle signals that emanate from a teacher also have a significant impact. Our inner state shows in skin color, muscular tension and posture, rate of breathing, eye movements, and so on. Teachers need to engage the interest and enthusiasm of students through their own enthusiasm, coaching, and modeling, so that the unconscious signals relating to the importance and value of what is being learned are appropriate. One reason it is important to practice what we preach and, for example, to be genuinely compassionate rather than to fake compassion, is that our actual inner state is always signaled and discerned at some level by others. Lozanov (1978) coined the term "double planeness" to describe this internal and external congruence in a person. In the same way, the design and administration of a school send messages to students that shape what is learned. In effect, every aspect of a student's life, including community, family, and technology, affects student learning.

8. Learning always involves conscious and unconscious processes.

We learn much more than we ever consciously understand. As Campbell (1989) has noted, "What we are discovering . . . is that beneath the surface of awareness, an enormous amount of unconscious processing is going on" (203). Most of the signals that are peripherally perceived enter the brain without the learner's awareness and interact at unconscious levels. Lozanov (1978) writes, "Having reached the brain, this information emerges in the consciousness with some delay, or it influences the motives and decisions" (18). We actually become our experiences and remember what we experience, not just what we are told. For example, a student can learn to sing on key and learn to hate singing at the same time. Teaching therefore needs to be designed in such a way as to help students benefit maximally from unconscious processing. In part, helping students benefit in this way is done by addressing the peripheral context (as described above); in part, it is done through instruction.

Implications for education: A great deal of the effort put into teaching and studying is wasted because students do not adequately process their experiences. What we call "active processing" allows students to review how and what they learn so that they begin to take charge of learning and the development of personal meanings. In part it refers to reflection and metacognitive activities. One example might be students becoming aware of their preferred learning style. Another might be the creative elaboration of procedures and theories by exploring metaphors and analogies to help reorganize material in a way that makes it personally meaningful and valuable.

9. **We have at least two different ways of organizing memory: a spatial memory system and a set of systems for rote learning.**
We have a natural, spatial memory system, which does not need rehearsal and allows for "instant" memory of experiences (Nadel and Wilmer 1980; Nadel, Wilmer, and Kurz 1984; Bransford and Johnson 1972). Remembering where we ate and what we had for dinner last night does not require the use of memorization techniques, because we have at least one memory system actually designed for registering our experiences in ordinary three-dimensional space (O'Keefe and Nadel 1978). The system is always engaged and is inexhaustible. It is possessed by people of both sexes and all nationalities and ethnic backgrounds. It is

enriched over time as we increase the items, categories, and procedures that we take for granted. (Thus, there was a time when we did not know what a tree or a television was.) This memory system is motivated by novelty. In fact this is one of the systems that drives the search for meaning mentioned in point three above.

Facts and skills that are dealt with in isolation are organized differently by the brain and need much more practice and rehearsal. The counterpart of the spatial memory system is a set of systems specifically designed for storing relatively unrelated information. Nonsense syllables are an extreme case. The more separated information and skills are from prior knowledge and actual experience, the more dependence there needs to be on rote memory and repetition. We can compare this memory system to the inventory of an automobile shop. The more items are available the more the shop can repair, build, and even design cars. It can also do so with greater ease and speed and less stress. At the same time, if management becomes too enamored of the stocking of inventory, and mechanics and designers fail to see how to use the materials available, then an imbalance has been created. In the same way, emphasizing the storage and recall of unconnected facts is a very inefficient use of the brain.

Implications for education: Educators are adept at the type of teaching that focuses on memorization. Common examples include multiplication tables, spelling words and unfamiliar vocabulary at the lower levels, and abstract concepts and sets of principles in different subjects for older students and adults. Sometimes memorization is important and useful. In general, however, teaching devoted to memorization does not facilitate the transfer of learning and probably interferes with the subsequent development of understanding. By ignoring the personal world of the learner, educators actually inhibit the effective functioning of the brain.

10. **We understand and remember best when facts and skills are embedded in natural, spatial memory.**

Our native language is learned through multiple interactive experiences involving vocabulary and grammar. It is shaped both by internal processes and by social interaction (Vygotsky 1978). The learning of language is an example of how specific "items" are given meaning when embedded in ordinary experiences. All education can be enhanced when this type of embedding is adopted. Such embedding is the single most important element the new brain-based theories of learning have in common.

Implications for education: The embedding process is complex because it depends on all the other principles discussed above. Spatial memory is generally best invoked through experiential learning, an approach that is valued more highly in some cultures than in others. Teachers need to use a large number of real-life activities, including classroom demonstrations, projects, field trips, visual imagery of certain experiences and best performances, stories, metaphor, drama, interaction of different subjects, and so on. Students can experience vocabulary, for example, through skits. They can learn grammar in process through stories or writing. Mathematics, science, and history can be integrated so that much more information is understood and absorbed than is presently the norm. Success depends on making use of all the senses and of orchestrating the immersion of a learner in a multitude of complex and interactive experiences. Lectures and analyses are not excluded, but they should be part of a larger experience.

11. **The brain downshifts under perceived threats and learns optimally when appropriately challenged.**

The brain will downshift under threat (Hart 1983), which involves a narrowing of the perceptual field (Combs and Snygg 1959). The learner becomes less flexible and reverts to automatic and often more primitive routine behaviors. It is roughly like a camera lens that has a reduced focus. The hippocampus, a part of the limbic system, which appears to function partially as a relay center to the rest of the brain, is the region of the brain most sensitive to stress (Jacobs and Nadel 1985). Under perceived threat, portions of our brain function suboptimally.

Implications for education: Teachers and administrators need to create a state of relaxed alertness in students. This state combines general relaxation with an atmosphere that is low in threat and high in challenge. The teacher must be in this state, and it must continuously pervade the lesson. All the methodologies that are used to orchestrate the learning context influence the state of relaxed alertness.

12. Each brain is unique.

Although we all have the same set of systems, including our senses and basic emotions, they are integrated differently in every brain. In addition, because learning actually changes the structure of the brain, the more we learn the more individual we become.

Implications for education: Teaching should be multifaceted in order to allow all students to express visual, tactile, emotional, or auditory preferences. There are other individual differences that also need to be taken into consideration. Choices should also be variable enough to attract individual interests. We can vary the choices in this way, but doing so may require the reshaping of schools so that they exhibit the complexity found in life. In sum, education needs to facilitate optimal brain functioning.

Notes

Discarding Outmoded Assumptions

These principles of learning based upon brain research move us inexorably beyond the information-processing model of memory as the paradigm for learning. For instance, an essential aspect of that model is the suggestion that we all have an information bottleneck. Of the wealth of information in the environment, the old model suggests that we can only place a small amount in short-term memory at any one time. We are further advised that long-term memory depends upon the processing and working of the contents of short-term memory. To the extent that we have limited learning to this scenario we have actually precluded ourselves from taking advantage of the greater capacities of the human brain.

Clearly we do have a limited capacity to focus attention. However, we indirectly perceive and respond to much that is happening in our total environment. Moreover, we process much in our environment unconsciously. The consequence is that our focus of attention becomes a tool, like a spotlight, but it is not nearly as limiting as we have been led to believe. Students are capable of much more learning and doing than we tend to expect, because everything is always operating in relationship to a much larger context.

What Educators Need to Do

Determining how to implement these principles is not a matter of preferring one specific methodology over another. As Madeline Hunter writes in a recent ASCD yearbook (Joyce 1990), "There are no teacher or student behaviors that have to be in every lesson. . . . We are . . . becoming sensitized to the appropriateness, artistry, and outcomes of what is occurring in the classroom. . . . This necessitates skill in selecting from a pharmacy of educational alternatives, not being committed to one 'best way'" (xiv). We all have access to an extensive societal repertoire of strategies and methods. What we need is a way of selecting what to use to maximize learning and make teaching more effective and fulfilling.

The first task is to view learning in terms of what the brain does. Most important, perhaps, is the conclusion that the brain is a social brain (Gazzaniga 1985). Individuals do not exist in isolation but in relationship to a dynamic and interactive world within which they continuously seek to position themselves and of which they want to make sense. Hence we must also reconceptualize learning outcomes in order to deal with primary importance of meaningfulness. We do that in chapter 4. It is an approach to education that recognizes the primacy of complex experience and regards learning as the art of capitalizing on experience. The three interactive elements of the process are then spelled out in the next chapter and are reviewed after the brain principles are experienced in depth.

That which is boundless in you
abides in the mansion of the sky,
whose door is the morning mist,
and whose windows are the songs and the silences of night.

— Kahlil Gibran, *The Prophet*

3

Your Learning Climate*

One reason change and restructuring are so difficult is that there are usually some conditions operating below the surface that interfere with what we do. It's like a gardener who works diligently to remove weeds from a flowerbed without eliminating the root systems. The bed may look wonderful, but after a while the weeds come back.

We became aware of some of these underlying conditions as we researched the nature of learning. The conditions are particularly important because many of the factors that inhibit learning in the classroom also operate in the larger world to frustrate organizational change. An important phenomenon that relates to this discussion is what Leslie Hart (1983) calls "downshifting." Research into the biological bases of memory, stress, anxiety, and creativity (among other fields) points to downshifting as a coherent phenomenon. There appear to be two interconnected types of downshifting—situational and long term. The details and sources are spelled out in *Making Connections*. In this book we will discuss some of the consequences of downshifting and explore our solution.

---

*This chapter is a modified and expanded version of an article by Geoffrey and Renate Caine published in *The Instructional Leader*, May 1991.

Notes

Downshifting

We downshift when we experience a threat that is accompanied by a sense of helplessness or fatigue. This feeling results in a reversion to deeply entrenched, early learned behaviors and programming, and to the sorts of primitive responses associated with the "fight or flight" response. We also find it difficult to perceive new opportunities, recognize context cues, and deal with uncertainty. Sometimes we even find it impossible to access ideas and procedures that we already know.

What Conditions Lead to Downshifting in the Classroom?

Although downshifting can be experienced in many ways, our own research indicates that the following set of conditions induces situational downshifting for the vast majority of students in the classroom.

1. **Prespecified "correct" outcomes have been established by an agent other than the learners.**
   This translates into the students' having to learn the answers the teacher has determined to be correct, which significantly narrows the options available to students. They are not in charge of their own learning and therefore feel helpless.

2. **Personal meaning is limited.**
   In other words, what is to be learned does not always connect with what students already know, which forces them into memorization, because the brain deals with unconnected information differently from the way in which it deals with "meaningless" information. Students' innovative or chosen ways of dealing with problems and situations are treated as irrelevant.

3. **Rewards and/or punishment are externally controlled and relatively immediate.**
   The consequences of action, including testing and grades, are not under the control of the students.

4. Restrictive time lines are given.

While deadlines are important in their place, a constant barrage of time limitations drives people to do what has to be done to meet the deadline, rather than to reflect on options or focus on the genuine parameters of the task.

5. Work to be done is relatively unfamiliar and little support is available.

Isolation exacerbates uncertainty and provides no reassurance that success is likely.

It is easy to see that these conditions contribute synergistically to a profound sense of helplessness for most students. It is this helplessness that induces downshifting. The conditions are situation specific, however. Students can feel different degrees of competence and helplessness in different contexts. It is also clear that people are different. Thus, some students perform very well in the conditions listed above. Sadly, some of our "best" students master this system and actually dislike open-ended and innovative approaches, which maximize the making of creative connections. Similarly, most of us would be too frightened to go into a cage of lions, but a few people thrive in the role of lion tamer.

A more general and pervasive type of downshifting can also occur. There are several contributing factors. One is the pervasive operation of the specific conditions mentioned above throughout a school or within the home. Another is a persistent sense of rejection and abandonment. A third factor is chronic fatigue. These can induce a sense of helplessness in life beyond the classroom.

What Happens When We Downshift?

1. We seek to protect ourselves.

In the classroom, self-protection translates into pleasing the teacher, which then translates into memorizing for the test rather than exploring and questioning in order to understand. The net effect is to inhibit rather than to encourage meaningful learning.

2. **We tend to have a significantly reduced capacity to adapt to new circumstances.**
   We tend to perseverate—to persist with set modes of behavior in a fairly rigid and unresponsive way. Students may therefore perpetuate ways of behaving and methods of study that manifestly do not work. In fact they tend not to respond to, and may not even perceive, substantial changes in the behavior of and signals from others.

3. **We revert to routines, procedures, and behaviors that have been deeply programmed, usually in childhood.**
   Examples include ignoring others, procrastination, avoidance, and overt impatience. Reversion to such routine behaviors is particularly harmful because what Karl Pribram calls "active uncertainty," which includes a capacity to tolerate ambiguity, is indispensable for meaningful learning.

4. **We revert to a set of very primitive instinctual behaviors having to do with preservation of our safety.**
   This reversion is an implication of Paul Maclean's theory of the triune brain. The result is that we bond very firmly to groups that are like minded. We also become territorial and adversarial, treating others as the enemy, which is a large contributor to the discipline problems that we find in school.

Implications for Restructuring

Change involves learning. Thus, the hidden conditions that inhibit learning in the classroom can also be expected to operate in the restructuring of an organization. While the circumstances vary from school to school and district to district, there are obvious common parallels to the classroom situation.

- Schools are often expected to take a specific shape and to provide quite specific results in the face of externally controlled tests and criteria of excellence. Test scores are a current example.

- Such requirements force many teachers to follow traditional methods of teaching at a time when innovation and risk taking are called for, because accountability carries with it the threat of severe punishment, including the threat of losing a job.

- Change necessarily involves uncertainty, with which many people are uncomfortable.

- There are always competing interest groups, and it is impossible to satisfy all of them.

- There is usually a sense of urgency and a felt need to accomplish a great deal in a very short time.

- There may be a distinct lack of community or administrative support.

- The methods and procedures favored by the teachers—the essence of what makes sense to them—are often disregarded by those with social, financial, and political power.

In sum, the conditions in which much restructuring must take place virtually guarantee that downshifting will occur.

What Conditions Reduce Downshifting?

Above all, participants need to feel safe as they experiment responsibly. We suggest that the following elements are needed. The conditions are the same in essence for classroom and for organizational change.

1. **Outcomes should be relatively open-ended.** This does not mean that anything goes. It means that we acknowledge and provide for the fact that there will be several possible solutions and not just one right answer.

2. **Personal meaning should be maximized.** The actual life experiences, styles, and understandings of individuals matter and are accommodated.

3. **Emphasis should be on intrinsic motivation.** Creativity and cooperation are fostered when people have a sense of ownership in the process. Students in the classroom and educators in the organization should all be participating because that is what they want to do.

4. **Tasks should have relatively open-ended time lines.** Learning and change are both developmental processes, and people and organizations develop at varying rates. The brain, for instance, does not work on fifty-five-minute cycles. Schools therefore need to look at flexible scheduling, which allows for more realistic learning and planning. In the long run, relative open-endedness will speed up both learning and change.

5. **Tasks should be manageable and supported.** An essential ingredient here is appropriate pacing, so that challenges are geared to available resources, an appropriate degree of difficulty, and moderate expectations. The most successful people tend to select moderately difficult tasks. They achieve excellence because their challenges are constantly upgraded—but always by manageable chunks.

Assessing Your Learning Climate

We invite you to answer the following questions about your place of work. This survey is very general, and your responses will be colored by your own state of mind at the moment. You may also answer differently at different times of the year. Nevertheless, the survey will provide you with a good general sense of the climate within which you work.

We have not weighted any question.

Select yes or no for each statement or phrase. Specific answers may not be critical, but generally, the more Ys you have in parts 1 and 2, the more likely that downshifting is occurring in the place in question. Note that in recording your responses, it does not matter how much control you have over the situation. In fact the less control or input you feel that you have, the more likely you are to be personally downshifted.

PART 1:
Factors that cumulatively indicate the existence of downshifting in the classroom

	Y	N
Letter or number grades are the primary means of evaluation	___	___
Curriculum is fragmented: subjects are separated from each other and from life outside the classroom	___	___
Organization is by age or grade level	___	___
Achievement is based on age- or grade-level criteria	___	___
Most outcomes are prespecified by teachers	___	___
There is a lack of focus on alternative answers and solutions	___	___
Intelligence is narrowly defined (for example, excessive emphasis on language and math)	___	___
Teachers show indifference to variety in learning styles	___	___
There is little group participation	___	___
Student groups are poorly developed	___	___
Staff shows indifference to students' interests and how they relate to subject matter	___	___
There is indifference to student experiences as rich sources of connection to the focus of the curriculum	___	___
Students are motivated through rewards and punishments	___	___
Class time is dominated by the teacher (a "delivery model" of teaching prevails)	___	___
There are constant interruptions (for example, bells, announcements)	___	___
Grades are the primary motivation for completing assignments	___	___
Time schedules govern learning tasks	___	___
There is lack of teacher planning time	___	___
Curriculum is "prescribed," not faculty generated or developed by faculty/educator teams	___	___
Total	___	___

PART 2:
Some symptoms of downshifting in the school as a whole

	Y	N
Staff is split into factions	___	___
There is extensive resistance to change	___	___
Negativity is extensive	___	___
There is limited concern for the system as a whole	___	___
Burn-out is common	___	___
There are few teacher teams or partnerships	___	___
Faculty is accountable but without power	___	___
Students are apathetic	___	___
Student absenteeism is high	___	___
Staff absenteeism is high	___	___
Total	___	___

PART 3:
Some factors that counter downshifting

	Y	N
Students participate in their own evaluations (including assessment of own strengths and weaknesses)	___	___
Students are given choices on tasks	___	___
Tasks are related to student goals, concerns, and interests	___	___
Tasks incorporate student experiences	___	___
Tasks include open-ended assignments	___	___
Student creativity is engaged and encouraged	___	___
Teachers help students process "deep meanings" (the impact on their own values, drives, purposes)	___	___
Many time lines are flexible and linked to activities	___	___

(continued)

Part 3:
Some factors that counter downshifting (continued)

	Y	N
There is time for student-teacher conferencing	___	___
There is time for teacher-teacher conferencing	___	___
There is time for teacher-student-parent conferencing	___	___
"Mistakes" are seen as a natural aspect of learning	___	___
Students share and work with each other	___	___
Students engage in reflection on content and on themselves (active processing)	___	___
Teachers engage in personal and professional reflection	___	___
Teachers share burdens and tasks and work together	___	___
Mutual respect and caring is nurtured in classrooms and the school	___	___
Codes of behavior and conduct are consistent and respected	___	___
Parents are actively involved in the school	___	___
Nonteaching staff members are openly respected and regularly acknowledged	___	___
New students are systematically welcomed into the school	___	___
New teachers are supported	___	___
The board and community support the school	___	___
Total	___	___

Clarifying Your Needs

Now take a moment to think about your current teaching environment and then think about how you would like your environment to be.

Make a partial list of some of the major problems facing you in your work. You can return to and modify this list from time to time.

Make a few preliminary notes on your ideal work environment as an educator. For example, what atmosphere would you like to have in your classroom and in your school? How would you like to relate to your colleagues? What would you like your students to be able to do?

How will you be able to tell when a specific goal or all your goals have been achieved?

Examples of indicators:

- You look forward to work each day.

- You finish the week tired but without feeling drained.

- Colleagues work together to solve problems.

- Students come to you with ideas for challenging projects.

Your indicators

We Indians think of the Earth and the whole universe as a neverending circle, and in this circle man is just another animal. The buffalo and the coyote are our brothers, the birds, our cousins. Even the tiniest ant, even a louse, even the smallest flower you can find—they are all relatives.

— Jenny Leading Cloud

4

Reconceptualizing Outcomes

We must be clear about what we need to accomplish in education. Irrespective of specific outcomes sought in specific courses or programs, what matters is the type of knowledge that is acquired. We need to go beyond the surface knowledge reflected in tests for memorization. The brain that connects information meaningfully does not just remember. It understands and relates to what is taught. A student who makes real sense of what is taught so that it can be used readily and easily in the ordinary world is acquiring natural knowledge.

Our primary goal in education must be to teach for the expansion of a student's natural knowledge.

Surface Knowledge

Those of us who visit classrooms, read textbooks, and listen to students see an educational system that has stripped much of the meaning out of the curricula and out of the process of learning. If we hear the statement "Today we are going to learn about the steamboat" or "about molecules" or "about *The Old Man and the Sea,*" we say to ourselves, "So what?" and wait to hear if our question is answered. Usually it is not. Instead, we often hear students complain, "Why do I have to learn that?" It doesn't matter that the material to be learned may be important later on; for them at that moment it seems useless. We speak about this kind of learning as "jumping through hoops."

This is what we call surface knowledge. It has no perceived value or real meaning for the learner. It is memorized for the test and then, almost invariably, forgotten. There is very little connectedness with other knowledge or with social and emotional issues or with other aspects of the learner's psyche. In the terms of the great philosopher Alfred North Whitehead, surface knowledge is "inert knowledge." Whitehead suggested that the greatest threat to education is inert knowledge. He is also reputed to have said that "knowledge doesn't keep any better than fish." Perhaps we have too many dead fish in our educational process.

Much education deals with the acquisition of surface knowledge—information that is unrelated to student goals or deeper understanding.

When have you been required to learn only surface knowledge?

How did you feel?

Do you ever teach like this?

Who or what influences you to teach like this?

Natural Knowledge

Natural knowledge is different from surface knowledge. Natural knowledge is all the knowledge that is second nature to us. It is at the heart of pattern recognition. It is what we think with rather than what we think about. It involves a degree of connectedness. It is all our knowledge that makes sense. It is what is actually understood.

Literacy as an Example of Natural Knowledge

In order to read well, we have to recognize letters, words, and sentences immediately. We also have a sense for how themes unfold and we know some of the important questions to ask.

We must have a sense of how a story "works," with a beginning, a middle, and an end. We have a basic idea of what characters do. We know that action occurs in a context, so we usually expect some description of the place where the action happens. We also know the difference between a novel, a textbook, and a newspaper.

When we read well, we call upon all of this knowledge simultaneously. We can do it in different contexts, with different material, for different purposes.

As an experiment, list some of the patterns that you take for granted when reading a newspaper. Example: The layout of sections and columns.

In a way, natural knowledge of a subject simply means being literate in that subject—being able to recognize essential patterns so that we can use the subject appropriately, which is why we can say that what an expert has is natural knowledge.

A musician can "read" the music and judge how well a particular orchestra is playing. An architect can "read" the state and style of a house. A politician can "read" the polls and transfer the results into "reading" the pulse of the electorate.

The Natural Knowledge We Already Have

One of the best examples of the natural knowledge that we all have is our native language. While our uses of formal grammar may vary, we all have a type of grammar. The range of different vocabularies is enormous, but we all have a substantial choice of words that make sense. Moreover, we can call upon our language in many different contexts to deal with many different situations, without having to think about how to speak.

Of course there are limits, but limits are in the nature of natural knowledge. It consists of what is currently second nature to us—and we all have some.

We know many things in ways similar to the way in which we know language. They include family and community rituals (from how to greet each other and the clothes we wear to the use of malls and the nature of holidays) as well as many of our hobbies, street wisdom, and so on.

Give some examples of your students' natural knowledge:

When the material that we deal with is sufficiently meaningful and is experienced in sufficiently complex ways, it becomes natural knowledge. We look at the world through the lens of what is second nature to us. It is that knowledge that we use to perceive the patterns of what is happening.

Every subject that students learn must be used to contribute to their natural knowledge—whether it is math, music, or economics. Only then will the knowledge be internalized in sufficient depth to be of practical value in a complex world.

Distinguishing between Surface Knowledge and Natural Knowledge

One of our biggest problems is that we have been blinded by an obsession with testing for behavioral objectives. We have therefore lost sight of the type of knowledge that we actually want students to acquire.

The reason is that tests, particularly those with multiple choice questions, tend to be tests of memorization. It is true that memorization can be quite complex. For example, we could learn how to "analyze the causes of war" and then write in substantial detail about the differences between the Vietnam War and the Gulf War. However, even this type of knowledge tends to be surface knowledge: it does not prepare a student to solve complex problems and apply the knowledge to unexpected and complex real-life situations.

Formal tests for specific performance and for memory are useful to some extent. However, relying on them too much reduces what teachers and learners do to encourage memorization. In fact, tests often interfere with a student's ability to understand work because they fail to allow for complexity of thought and an intuitive grasp of situations.

The knowledge for understanding work and grasping ideas intuitively is natural knowledge. It must be assessed in context, using the sorts of methods that adequately reflect a complex world.

The best way to demonstrate the acquisition of natural knowledge is to identify the ways in which natural knowledge manifests itself in ordinary life. We can then use these manifestations to create a set of indicators that tell us what sort of knowledge students are acquiring.

Example: To what extent would students who have "learned to analyze the causes of war" be able to

Analyze the nature of gang conflict and urban warfare?

Respond differently from the way they currently respond to conflict in their own class, school, or society?

Indicators of the Acquisition of Natural Knowledge

Here is a checklist that you can use as indicators of the acquisition of natural knowledge.

Which of the following do your students show?

✔ The ability to use the language of the discipline or subject in complex situations and in social interaction.

✔ The ability to perform appropriately in unanticipated situations.

✔ The ability to solve real problems using the skills and concepts of any discipline or subject.

✔ The ability to show, explain, or teach the idea or skill to another person who has a real need to know.

✔ The ability to examine consciously and deliberately their performance in those different contexts and to appreciate their own strengths and weaknesses with respect to the subject matter in question.

IIII➡ CAUTION

There are many levels of natural knowledge. Thus, a person may be at home with reading short stories and yet not know how to read social studies texts. A person may also be moderately expert with word processors and yet not be at all at home with other computer software.

In developing your indicators, always be aware of the degree of student sophistication with which you are dealing. The important goal is to teach for the expansion of natural knowledge at every level of education in which understanding and meaningfulness are important.

Teaching for Meaning

We help students expand natural knowledge by teaching for meaning.

It has been said that the thing that most distinguishes humans from other animals is that we seek and create meaning from our experiences in the world. We ask questions such as *Why? How?* and *What?* in order to understand the world around us and our own unique place in it. We try to generate a record of the past to determine where we came from and what happened to the people who lived before us. We develop languages that help us communicate with others about what we think and how we feel. We create music and songs that somehow capture a sense of beauty, passion, and elegance. We create other artforms that allow us to reenact our experience in the world or to express a deep emotion. Humans also try to understand their environment, how it works, and how it came to be. We organize, categorize, label, and relate to our world. We have to try to make sense of it all.

Let's apply this tendency to try to make sense of our world to elementary students who are studying "explorers of the New World." Usually this study involves learning the names of the explorers, the geography of the regions, and some of the historical incidents that occurred. Creative teachers often have students actively involved in studying and learning the material. But where are the connectedness to our lives and the meaning and purpose that make learning about explorers important? For example, what does it mean to be an explorer? How does it feel? Is there fear? Excitement? Confusion? To what extent do we "own" what is discovered? How do we try to understand what is new, unseen, and unnamed? What does it mean to explore electricity? To explore peace? To explore relationships? To explore ourselves? Can animals and plants explore? What are different ways of exploring? Can we really explore anything without ultimately exploring ourselves? That is, what are our questions, our motives, our unknowns, our interests, and our feelings? How can exploring be celebrated and re-created as something common to all of life? The subject matter may be explorers, but the potential meanings are unbounded.

The world becomes meaningful (full of meaning) when we feel connected to it. "Content" is not some final outcome or set of isolated facts; rather it is the relationship of those facts to other facts, to our experience, to the human condition, and to the particular meanings we ascribe to them. Teaching for meaning challenges us to provide experiences for our students that encourage their own self-awareness as learners. What and how they learn is connected to the meanings they create.

Meaning can also provide us with a sense of purposefulness and a clearer sense of direction. In this way, it goes beyond merely understanding something. The individual creates meaning as a personalized response to experience. Meaning is thus constructed uniquely and has ramifications far beyond the understanding of a singular experience. When meaning is applied to learning, each learner is an integral part of what is being learned. Once this concept is recognized, the value of learners being aware of themselves as learners, as persons who creatively construct and organize meaning, is indispensable to the teaching process. Helping students become self-conscious or self-aware or mindful learners is part of what teaching for meaning is all about.

Our approach to teaching for meaning begins with thinking differently about what we do. We believe that when such a change occurs, the practical questions change and teachers respond creatively to new or expanded questions. The common orientation to curriculum and instruction has been to treat content in isolated fragments. This tacitly denies the connectedness that is evident all around us. When we perceive the world as whole and begin to explore how things are interrelated, we confer a sense of meaning and order to what we are studying. When we include the learner as an active participant in what is being learned, we have the basis for an educational practice that accentuates meaning.

As you explore the principles of brain-based learning, the connectedness between meaning and learning will become more apparent. Remember that connectedness is natural—it is everywhere and in everything. We have only to look for it. As our perceptions change, so will our practice.

Outcomes and skilled performance are extremely important. It is their importance to us as educators—their meaning for us—that drives what we do and what we teach. Similarly, students can meet basic objectives, and do much more, when what they are doing is meaningful to them. It must make sense. The outcomes are also better because meaningfulness naturally enhances memory and performance!

Expansion of Natural Knowledge Means Expansion of the Self

Real expansion of natural knowledge actually changes the learner because it changes the configuration of the self. The self is the sum total of who we are as unique individuals. It includes our autobiographical memories, our beliefs about how the world works, and the beliefs we hold about our own abilities and limitations.

The self needs consistency and, in many ways, tends to resist change because most people prefer not to have their personal definitions and beliefs challenged. Surface knowledge satisfies this need not to change. It consists of memories that do not significantly modify a person's outlook on life. Expansion of natural knowledge, on the other hand, engages the entire learner.

All our mind/body systems are involved in meaningful learning. The expansion of natural knowledge involves the entire spectrum of human experience, including emotions, physical responses, cognitive information, and social interaction. The various systems may not be working together. They may not be working effectively. But they are working.

Real learning—meaningful learning—actually changes a person. From a psychological perspective, the self is actually modified. From a physiological perspective, the brain is actually modified. These matters are not for debate; they are what happens.

The self might not be enhanced in school. On the contrary, it can be impoverished and diminished if it has inappropriate experiences. The only question, then, is whether the learner's experiences will enhance, diminish, or maintain the self.

Our capacity for the expansion of natural knowledge, like the number of possible connections between neurons, is virtually infinite. However, the educational process must be both orderly and exciting, immensely safe and yet infinitely challenging.

Teaching for meaning requires us to rethink the teaching/learning process and engage in a search for a new concept of teacher. It may also lead us to search for a new concept of school.

Notes

There is a catch, of course. There is a fundamental difference between teaching for specific performance and behavioral objectives on the one hand and teaching for meaning on the other. The latter is more complex, more subtle, less mechanical, more dynamic, more alive. It is "messier," but there is order of a complex kind. Teaching for meaning is different. We still have a curriculum of information and skills, but it can be connected to meaningful questions and experiences.

Teaching for meaning requires a major mind shift.

We hope the principles and ideas provided in this workbook give each of us legitimate reasons to make courageous decisions about the ways in which we practice education or to enhance what we already do. Collectively we can create a better tomorrow.

Preview: How to Teach for the Expansion of Natural Knowledge

Every system and approach that fosters teaching for the expansion of natural knowledge has three interactive elements:

- *Orchestrated immersion* of the learner in multiple, complex, interactive experiences. The experiences are much like those we all have as we learn our native language.

- A state of mind that we call *relaxed alertness*. At a minimum, this state of mind involves low threat and high challenge on the part of both educators and students.

- *Active processing* of experience, which means engaging in the testing, reflective, and meta-cognitive processes that allow us to extract more meaning from experience.

We will revisit these three elements after you have had an opportunity to explore the principles in depth. We will then offer a first model of how to teach for meaning. We begin by drawing from the way we all learned our native language. Those activities and experiences can be replicated in any subject, in part because every subject is also (but never exclusively) a language. We also provide a set of indicators that you can use to examine the extent to which meaningful learning is taking place. Please remember, however, that for the time being these indicators are to serve as much for your own learning and self-observation as for guidance in education.

Being open and being attentive is more effective than being judgmental. This is because people naturally tend to be good and truthful when they are being received in a good and truthful manner.

— John Heider, *The Tao of Leadership*

5

Guidelines for Process Groups

As success clearly depends upon addressing the underlying conditions that govern learning and change, we need to do that directly and immediately, from the very beginning. We have developed a process that seeks to deal with those hidden conditions.

Our goal is to form a genuine learning community. Every member of the staff, from principal and teachers to custodians and clerical and food service staff, is therefore invited to participate. We begin by forming self-directed study and process groups in which staff members directly explore the nature of learning and the hidden conditions that affect both learning and change.

Small groups meet for one or two hours, three times every four weeks, for five months. We link with one school whose staff are meeting on their own time and without compensation. All members of staff participate in a group. Every week each group explores some aspect of learning and one of our brain principles by means of exercises and activities we have included in *MindShifts*. The group may also investigate some additional readings, which they select, on the general area of restructuring. Teachers also observe and search for connections to what they themselves are learning in their classes during the week and report back to their groups in order to discuss experiences and results.

For this preliminary five-month period there are absolutely no outcome-based goals. That means that there is learning without failure. There is joint risk taking and mutual support.

Notes

Obviously there will be a need for attention to instruction, curriculum, and other issues, usually at a later date. However, the essence of our approach is to generate a significant amount of personal growth in the participants, to create a more profound sense of a learning community, and then to have their insights about learning and their sense of community drive the transformation of the school. As participants learn, they begin to work out their own vision of what an ideal school should look like. Part of the challenge, the fun, and the excitement for the staff is that they will create that new system for themselves, working together.

▶ CAUTION

As change and learning are nonlinear, the process is much messier than it first appears. For example, as we set out to deal with school climate and mental models, some curriculum innovations will emerge very quickly as soon as teachers with different areas of expertise begin to work together. Many changes will occur, often at unpredictable times. In addition, there will always be glitches. The goal, however, is to maintain the underlying conditions that make change both desirable and possible. It is a joy to work with people who share that philosophy. We believe that there is also a significantly higher likelihood of success.

Specific Objectives

There are at least four ongoing objectives for the process groups.

1. **Developing a learning community**
   Every classroom and school needs to be a context in which individuals support a group that nourishes individuals. Your explorations with this study group will both facilitate your own learning and assist in transforming the entire school into a learning community.

2. **Acquiring a sense of orderliness and process**
Meaningful learning requires a dynamic atmosphere that combines safety with excitement. One crucial foundation for this atmosphere is some taken-for-granted sense of timing and rhythm that is revealed, in part, in enhanced mutual respect and courtesy. Vocal interaction, for instance, is sometimes important and sometimes disruptive. Such orderliness and awareness of the process are best established through mutual understanding and not through rules enforced by punishment.

3. **Internalization of a theory of learning**
One of the best ways to develop a felt meaning for and to internalize new material is to create a context in which it is explored and discussed naturally. During this group process you will have many opportunities to explore the way in which the human brain learns, both through a series of group activities and through guided observation and reflection about what goes on in your class and in your school. In this way you will begin to internalize a mental model of learning that will be vital in assisting you to navigate the turbulent waters of educational change.

4. **Developing the habits and skills of reflection**
Almost all reflection and thought in schools focus on solving problems and dealing with what will happen in the future. At the heart of powerful education, however, is the constant reflection upon what has been learned from what has already happened. Through these groups you will be able to modify the habits of mind that interfere with reflection as well as acquire additional tools for capitalizing more fully on past experiences.

The point to realize is that groups evolve in a way similar to that in which people learn. It is not all clear sailing. There may be frustrations in getting started, disagreements about procedures, a degree of turbulence

Notes

and confusion, and even a degree of impatience. After all, we are under severe pressure to get things done, to achieve results, and generally to become perfect "yesterday."

The groups are important precisely because they are designed to counter those pressures while serving our goals. When they are given time and are respected, the groups tend to help us develop the basic conditions within which genuine growth and change become possible. You will find that mutual respect, a sense of orderliness and coherence, and a positive rhythm and routine are indispensable to the sorts of transformations that we all seek.

You will also find that many people who were initially reluctant end up with the greatest enthusiasm. Do not be dismayed by participants who seem to be dragging their heels. What matters is that the integrity of the process itself is maintained, which means that all participants adhere to the protocols and guidelines that are established.

In this chapter we describe a series of procedures that work very well. However, there is a constant dance between these guidelines and the choices and decisions that suit individual groups. Thus we find that each group tends to develop a personality of its own.

Getting Started

The first step is simply to get the groups started and to gain an overview and initial sense of what will be involved.

Preliminary Gathering(s)

In our experience, groups work most effectively when people buy in and commit themselves. Hence, we do not recommend any forced or imposed group participation. The members of the group will have varying degrees of background information, expertise, and interest. We suggest that you allow a significant amount of time to examine some basic ideas and explore shared values and purposes. It will help, working alone or together, for potential members to read the introduction and part 1 of this book. In these sections we ask several questions, and before beginning to meet is a good time to answer them and discuss your answers.

The goal is not only to be proficient in the ideas or the theory but to become familiar with the basic ideas and objectives that are being explored.

How to Create Groups

There are many ways to establish groups.

- A few friends or colleagues might agree to meet on a regular basis.

- The groups may be formed as the result of a more elaborate and formal process. For instance, in our approach to school restructuring, the first major two-day workshop has, as its outcome, the creation of process groups that involve as many members of the entire school staff as possible.

- The formation of process groups may be discussed and decided upon at a series of regular staff meetings.

After you have formed your groups, you will spend some time developing your own protocols, deciding when and where to meet, testing some of the basic strategies, and getting to know each other. You will also be doing some preliminary reading. In particular you should skim through this book so that you have an impression of the overall approach. You might like to cover all of these steps in one long meeting, or you might prefer to meet on two or three occasions to finish the preliminaries.

Facilitator

The person you choose to organize the groups should have prestige within the school and, ideally, have some experience with group dynamics. His or her role will be to work with members of the staff to implement these guidelines. The facilitator may be, but does not need to be, the principal. What matters is that people treat the process and the facilitator with respect.

Notes

Decisions that Need to Be Made

There are several initial issues about which you must make decisions.

- **Size of group:** You need to have enough people to keep the group interesting and alive, yet have few enough so that everyone has a significant opportunity to participate. In general, the longer your group meeting, the larger you can make your group. However, we suggest that a group of from five to eight people is ideal.

- **Membership:** We strongly recommend that your group contain some people who do not work together very closely on a regular basis so that there is a wider variety of input and experience. Of course, you will probably all be colleagues and have regular contact with each other. However, much of the power of the group comes from gaining insight into people who are different from you. In our restructuring program, we therefore tend to integrate the teaching and nonteaching staff.

- **Leadership:** The goal is for everyone to be both a leader and a follower. Meeting this goal is critical in establishing mutual respect and in overcoming the tendency for social and professional status to interfere with genuine communication. In the early stages some natural leaders will tend to stand out. Sometimes, leaders will be selected by the facilitator from a pool of volunteers. When working with an entire school, we ask the principal to select some leaders initially who have good prestige and leadership skills in order to launch the process. However, it is vital that some of the leadership rotate on a regular basis.

  Similarly, when groups are launching informally or without outside facilitation, we would expect natural leaders to take charge in the early stages. However, we strongly recommend that leadership of some processes begin to rotate fairly soon.

- *Venue:* A convenient and suitable venue needs to be selected, possibly at school or in a public meeting room. If either is your choice, we suggest some transition time because being in a school can often lead to focusing on problems or events of the day that are too tempting to ignore and take too long to process.

  The venue can also be a private home. If a home is offered, the home owner should NOT feel under immense obligation to cater lavishly. It might also be a good idea to move to a different home every now and then. Although some people like to meet in a restaurant, we feel that doing so will significantly change the way in which the group functions and is not a good idea. In particular, there will be distractions and interruptions that interfere with developing the sense of orderliness that we are seeking.

- *Time:* Members of the group need to commit to a sufficient period of time. We suggest two hours a week for at least three weeks out of every month. However, we understand that only one hour a week may be possible. In addition, every member needs to commit to a minimum amount of preparation, involving such reading and action as the group decides.

Guideline for Preliminary Gathering(s)

Show respect for each other. Everyone must have an opportunity to participate and be heard. All members should do their best to ensure that this occurs. The facilitator should make a point of making it possible for all to participate while keeping the gathering focused on the issues and task at hand.

Individual Differences

The members of the group will provide support and help in your commitment to the group. However, the group will

Notes

consist of people with different beliefs, goals, and styles, which will be immensely valuable in the long run because a wide variety of input, attitudes, and ideas will greatly increase your understanding and will be of benefit to you.

Of course, the differences can also be frustrating. Some people are precise about being on time and following guidelines, and others think that deadlines are meant to be changed and that guidelines are made to be ignored. Both styles are important; extremes of both are counterproductive.

We therefore suggest that one function of the preliminary gathering(s) should be to explore individual differences. This exploration will help you understand each other better, and it will enable you to appreciate and stick to those aspects of the guidelines that really are important to the process that we have developed.

In appendix B, we describe four different perceptual styles, which are derived from our own experience and from the work of many others. The styles have also been tested in schools, with children as well as teachers. They will prove to be of great value to you as you embark upon the change process.

Feel free to use other instruments and profiles and to discuss other characteristics that may be the basis of individual differences. Indeed, this topic could be explored from time to time during your entire group experience. You will find that you gain enormous insight into your students and their learning styles as well as into yourselves, your colleagues, and members of the community.

Group Guidelines

The membership, venue, and other aspects of your group have been decided. You have also overviewed the material and the process. You are now ready to embark. You should commit to at least two months, and ideally could commit for the entire year.

A learning community needs both spontaneity and routine. We therefore suggest that every meeting involve some combination of the following:

1. **A degree of routine and ceremony with beginnings and endings**

   "Learn to recognize beginnings. At birth, events are relatively easy to manage. Slight interventions can shape and guide easily. Potential difficulties can be avoided" (Heider 1985, 127).

   - *A way to begin:* You could start each meeting with a moment, say one minute, of total and restful silence. Perhaps begin with some relatively brief relaxation exercise, which might range from stretching to the use of selected music.

   - *A way to end:* There are two components here that we find very useful.

     First, take a moment to reflect on what happened and what you learned from this group experience. We suggest that each person in turn briefly share some personal insight. This process is not a time for competition, discussion, or debate, but merely a time to share what each has learned. It is important to observe the entire meeting and to note when there was a sense of togetherness and when there was a sense of disturbance and lack of togetherness. You then have an opportunity to reflect on the causes in you, in others, in the group, and in the larger context.

     Second, you may want to close with a simple ceremony. A song is one possibility; a moment of silence is another; "1-2-3 clap" is a third. For the last, you stand in a circle (like a huddle in football). Then together say out loud "one, two, three." Then clap. It should sound like one loud clap. This is usually a sign that people are focused.

2. **Time for "ordered" sharing about a selected topic**

   Here, each person has roughly the same amount of time to speak, and everyone participates. No one is judged or debated because every opinion is to be genuinely heard and valued. A mode of discussion is selected that allows for the development of a sense of order, continuity, and momentum. You should have a facilitator and timekeeper for this process. Make sure that everyone has an equal opportunity (as much as possible) to take these roles.

Note: The process for ordered sharing is described in detail in appendix A. Using this process is indispensable to the success of the groups and to your meeting your objectives.

There are at least two different types of content for use in this process.

- For groups that will meet for two hours at a time, the content that you use should be brief and profound. You might like to select the principle or big idea with which each of the chapters on the brain principles begins.

Examples are

The whole is greater than the sum of the parts.

Reality is both linear and nonlinear.

Inner and outer reflect each other.

Order is present everywhere.

Reality consists of matter, energy, and meaning.

Everything is part and whole simultaneously.

What is, is always in process.

Everything comes in layers.

Stable systems resist change; dynamic systems exist by changing.

Everything is connected.

Rhythms and cycles are present everywhere.

The whole is contained in every part.

Alternatively, you could select a brief poem, a short set of pithy readings or quotes, or a work of art. Here is an example:

From this hour I ordain myself loos'd of limits and
imaginary lines,
Going where I list, my own master total and absolute,
Listening to others, considering well what they say,
Pausing, searching, receiving, contemplating,
Gently, but with undeniable will, divesting myself of
the holds that would hold me.

— Walt Whitman, *"Song of the Open Road"*

- For groups that will meet for one hour at a time, use the brain principles themselves. At each meeting you will begin by using the process of ordered sharing to express your own view about the brain principle that will be examined during the rest of that meeting. Each person will have an opportunity to express an opinion as to what the idea means.

This process will serve two additional ends. First, these "big ideas" create a larger context within which your discussions will be found to be more meaningful. Second, they preexpose you to emerging developments in curriculum (which we call "the curriculum of wholeness"). For instance, you will find that many current teaching strategies such as thematic teaching and the integrated curriculum begin to fit together better as you master the messages embedded in the big ideas.

3. **Examination of the brain principles and other material**
   Since one of the key objectives is the development of a new mental model of learning, every group meeting in the first few months should be devoted, in part, to the exploration of at least

Notes

one of the brain principles. You will find each principle developed in depth, with a set of exercises, in part 2 of this workbook.

Other material can also be examined, though you will tend to do so when the exploration of the brain principles has been completed. We suggest, for instance, that each week you may select some key reading from leading books or journals.

During most of this discussion, people need to feel free to participate or not as they wish. Participation can involve argument and debate as well as reflections and mutual problem solving. This phase will not be as orderly as the getting started phase. However, there must be respect for all and opportunity for all to participate.

4. **Other topics**

These groups provide a perfect opportunity to discuss critical issues or experiments that you would like to try out in your work. One way to address these topics is for a different person to be given some time each week to discuss something of importance. This time can be used to report on how a strategy worked, to ask for advice, or to deal with some other issue. You could even use the time to test jointly some of the exercises and activities that you will find at the back of this workbook.

5. **Safety**

These groups must be psychologically safe. Each participant should make a commitment that nothing personal shared by any other participant will be made public without that person's consent. Every participant must publicly acknowledge that he or she will adhere to that commitment. Deciding whether or not to participate in a group is a delicate process. The most basic requirement is trust.

Shared Leadership

Different groups have different leadership needs. What is important is for everyone to experience being a leader as well as a follower. We suggest that one person be elected or appointed to get the ball rolling on the first night. At that time, other decisions can be made:

- Someone should assume responsibility for communicating with all the members, particularly if arrangements need to be changed. This role can be shared if you like.

- Someone should be chosen to facilitate the various processes. One way to do this is to appoint someone as group leader for a period of, say, a month and then rotate leadership. Another is to have a different leader every week.

Hints

1. **Be aware of the energy and focus of the group.**
   Energy dissipates very quickly if people come and go when they wish. Hence there should be an agreed-upon starting and finishing time, and it should be adhered to as much as possible. We suggest that you start each group on time, even if everyone has not yet arrived. Late arrivals should wait for a process to finish before moving in to join the group.

2. **Maintain personal journals through the week.**
   Select something of personal importance to share with the group. You might discuss the time you have chosen to discuss new procedures in class and explore the results.

3. **Do not give each other advice.**
   You will probably be enormously tempted to do this, but giving each other advice is NOT what this group is about. The goal is for people to learn from their own experience. Of course, sometimes you may want advice. Do not ask for it if you don't want it. Stop the process if you don't like the advice.

Notes

4. **Maintain the process.**

At times people may feel euphoric. At other times people may feel low. Such mood changes are just a part of life. They are also quite natural when we change our mental models. One of the functions of the group is to develop a feel for continuity of the learning process and for the power of a sense of community, no matter what we are feeling. Such continuity and power will help you enormously in your change process.

Keys to Restructuring

1. **Your group process will tend to reflect the dynamics of change.**

Here are some possible experiences. They are natural and part of the process.

- There may be enthusiasm at first, with some people resisting more than others.

- The group and the process may feel strange for a while.

- There will usually be a significant point at which confusion turns to comfort and uncertainty turns to enthusiasm.

- After a while things may become routine to the point that you do not want any change—even though later changes may be important.

- You may also find that you have bonded with certain members of the group to the point that other members tend to be excluded.

Remember that looking at what is happening and moving beyond "blocks" is part of the challenge.

2. **Gather with other groups on occasion.**

At least once every two months or so, gather with the members of other groups to reflect on the process, on what you have learned, and how it all connects with your larger goals—from instructional change to total restructuring. This meeting should be facilitated by someone within the school who commands a great deal of natural prestige and who clearly understands the process. It can be a partially structured meeting. For instance, there could be a set of questions developed and handed out that all answer. There could be some open-ended discussion. You could use one of the processes or strategies that you have been testing. Remember that this meeting CAN be part of a normal planning meeting or staff meeting. If that is how you intend to run it, however, be sure to include all nonteaching staff who have been participating in the groups.

Anticipate Change

At some time, perhaps at the end of a year, this phase of group work will come to an end. New groups can then be formed that have more functions and purposes in common. There is no need to plan those groups at this stage, but it does help to be aware that the new groups will be formed. Other changes are bound to be introduced. The bottom line is simply to maintain the process and the groups for a significant amount of time so that your mental models of learning take hold and the underlying atmosphere of a learning community begins to unfold.

PART II

Principles of
Brain-Based Learning

It is the letting go that is difficult.
The questions and concepts and knowledge of a lifetime
Hang on to me as a tether of a
Bungi cord.
I want my expansion to be unimpaired,
The magnet of the earth's center unimpeded.
Then truth can be known.

The whole is greater than the sum of its parts

6

Principle One

The Brain Is a Parallel Processor

In *Making Connections,* we acknowledged and introduced the complexity of the brain by likening it to a city in the mind. In a city, there are always many things happening at one time. Utilities are operating. The media are at work. Government, education, business, and transport are functioning, even though there may be times of high and low activity. Our brains are equally active, with a vast number of simultaneous processes taking place. That is why we call it a parallel processor.

We suffer from an enormous handicap in education. It is the belief that the brain does one thing at a time. For instance, we tend to believe that

- a student can learn only one thing at a time

- a student learns only when paying attention

- the amount of time spent "on task" is the most important factor in learning.

All of these beliefs are open to debate. The reason for questioning their truth is summed up in the statement that the brain is a parallel processor.

We will focus on four aspects of parallel processing that affect learning and teaching:

1. The complex nature of attention

2. The development of an autobiographical memory

3. Survival and health: ongoing physiological processes

4. Building interpersonal and social relations

The Complex Nature of Attention

When we pay attention, perhaps to a conversation or a game, we seem to be devoting all our energy and resources to that event. In fact, much more is happening.

Activity

Find an object in the room, such as a plant or chair, and begin to observe it closely. As you observe the object you selected, ask yourself:

- What percent of my field of vision does it occupy?

- What else can I observe out of the "sides" of my eyes?

- What sounds can I hear, now that I have decided to be on the lookout for them?

- What information are my other senses picking up?

- What messages are coming to me from "inside"?

Commentary

You are directly paying attention to the object of choice. In addition, you are indirectly attending to many other signals, such as sounds in the room or the movement of people around you. All the stimulation that you indirectly respond to is part of your peripheral perception.

This peripheral awareness is critical to such things as your ability to hear, to stand upright, and to know when to get out of someone's way. Your brain is constantly monitoring the global environment at the same time that you are paying attention to a specific object or person or process.

A good illustration of this phenomenon is when you are on a long trip with a friend and you are doing the driving. Have you ever found yourself so engrossed in a discussion that you suddenly realized that you had driven many miles without being aware of it?

Driving demands constant adjustment to many factors, including the behavior of other traffic, the weather, and your destination. Much of the adjustment is automatic, below the threshold of what we call "paying attention." This example illustrates the fact that we can perceive and respond to some inputs at the same time that we are concentrating on something else. Even in what appears to be the simple fact of paying attention, there is much more happening in our brains than we can ever maintain in our awareness.

The Development of an Autobiographical Memory

In addition to whatever activity has your attention, and in addition to monitoring the environment, your brain is also recording a total experience. Without knowing it, you are organizing and storing an enormous number of signals and stimuli in the form of an ongoing auto-biographical memory.

Activity

Next time you go shopping or go to a movie or to school, spend a few moments afterward recollecting as much as you can of the events that led up to your activity. Here are some illustrative questions.

- Whom were you with?

- What was the weather like?

- How did you travel?

- Where did you park (if you parked)?

- What sort of mood were you in?

Notes

Commentary

Laughter, funny gestures, and frustrating incidents are being absorbed on many levels (emotional, physical, interpersonal) and the entire procedure is recorded in memory. It is part of the ongoing story of your life. In a similar way, every student is continuously developing a life story.

Thus in a very real way, students are learning some things all the time. Their autobiographical memory is recording entire experiences, which contribute to the creation of an identity.

We will deal with autobiographical memory in much more depth in chapter 14.

Survival and Health: Ongoing Physiological Processes

Although we may become conscious of issues of health and survival only occasionally, we are always dealing with them. The body needs to be maintained: food needs to be digested, blood needs to circulate, and the immune system needs to protect the body from illness.

Activity

In an earlier activity, we asked you to find an object and observe it closely. As you did, which bodily systems were involved? Separate your answers into two types. Which systems do you simply know were involved? Which systems could you actually perceive?

- Were you breathing? How hard?

- Was your heart pumping? How fast?

- Were you aware of where you were in the room?

- Were you emotional in any way—happy, embarrassed, challenged, irritated?

- Was your body maintaining its temperature?

- Was your immune system operating?

- What other systems could be included?

What you know happens	What you actually perceive or experience

You'll probably have more items in the "What you know" column. That is simply because we tend to know more information about ourselves than what we are actually aware of from moment to moment.

Commentary

Our brains are monitoring every system during every waking and sleeping moment. The fact that we may not be aware of many of our more anatomical processes is not important (and frequently awareness is impossible and not helpful), but in many instances we do need to learn to monitor our bodily reactions better. One reason is that learning engages all these processes, as we will see.

When we talk about increasing awareness we mean becoming more conscious of what we are experiencing. This increased consciousness will turn out to be extremely important as you begin to design learning environments that are brain compatible, and it is also why this book provides so many experiences for you. Becoming aware of your own feelings, beliefs, and other elements of experience will help to solidify and give meaning to the content that we teach.

Notes

Building Interpersonal and Social Relations

In almost everything we do that involves others, complex social and interpersonal relationships are evolving.

Activity

Observe, or spend a few moments remembering, children in a playground at school. You may like to think back over a period of several days or weeks. Do you see any evidence of any of the following?

- Competition for attention, for dominance

- Groups of cliques forming and being maintained

- Kids taking what appear to be foolish risks

- Individuals or groups congregating in the same general area

- Ideas and experiences from other times being introduced into discussion (such as what happened in class or on TV)

- Lots of movement and shifting of position

Commentary

What you are observing are all the hallmarks of complex societies in operation. Groups are bonding, people are being socialized, territory is being invaded and protected, egos are being challenged and defended, relationships are being formed, and so on. These are the subject of disciplines as varied as sociology, psychology, history, anthropology, and biology.

What is interesting is that all of these developments are taking place during the playing of a game. Moreover, they are taking place even though attention seems to be on the game itself!

In fact, you are observing another level of brain and mind operation that is occurring simultaneously. (You may want to look at chapter 5 in *Making Connections*). Our brains and minds are working at multiple levels and in many different and complex ways—all at the same time.

The students may have been attending to one issue, but they have been learning an enormous amount indirectly, most of which they did not intend to learn.

Now, let's translate that phenomenon into the classroom. Instead of a game, the student is supposed to be learning math or language. Even though the context has changed, the same large range of issues will be alive in the student's mind. The issues include

- The need for social rituals

- The need to use language and express choice

- The need to be recognized and perhaps to move up or down in the pecking order

- The need for safety, order, and socially imposed limits

- The need to master strategies and acquire relevant information

Traditional teaching tends to separate these developments from the examination of content, such as math or language. Brain-based education combines and uses them.

Implications for Teaching

These multiple processes will be as present in a learning environment as in any other life activity. Learners will engage in them. They all support each other in a healthy environment. Thus, the budding friendships among the students help them to appreciate the rules of the game, and talk and movement are all directly related to learning a game as well as to bonding. The processes are all involved in some ways, therefore, in the construction of natural knowledge. We cannot stop them; we can only direct them. Such direction is the reason people use such procedures as cooperative learning.

We must take advantage of the brain's innate capacities and of all those different tendencies. We are not suggesting that you need to duplicate all that happens on a playground. We are suggesting that all teachers need to capitalize on the processes and developments that can be found in real life. When we grasp the complexity of the brain and design lessons and other work accordingly, we begin to automatically engage the mind/body systems in appropriate ways without having to deal with each separately.

We will go into detail later. For the time being, here are some questions to guide you:

How is a lecture different from student participation in a large, real-life project?

Do you work to create groups in which students can work together?

Do you ever discuss what happens to them during breaks and after school and relate it to the topic of the day?

Do students have permission to go off on creative tangents at times? Can you relate these tangents to the learning focus?

What could you do to create the same atmosphere in a classroom that students have when learning games privately?

Complex systems are both linear and nonlinear

7

Principle Two

Learning Engages the Entire Physiology

It is sometimes said that the mind is in the body and the body is in the mind. That is correct. All mental processes, including learning, are substantially influenced by our physiology. In this discussion we will explore two different but interconnected aspects of this relationship:

1. **There is a complex interaction between health, attitude, and learning capacity.**
   We all know that it is hard to study when we are sick. The same is true of learners under the influence of drugs or alcohol. Moreover, some of the pressures of a school life can actually make people ill. Did you know that college students going through final exams have demonstrated depressed immune functioning? Their lowered Helper T Cell count results in colds and flu for many of them.

2. **We use the body to construct knowledge.**
   For example, in Principle One we talked about forming autobiographical memories. Our senses are an indispensable part of that process and, indeed, of the process of learning almost anything.

Health, Attitude, and Capacity

At one time, a compartmentalized view of the human body and mind was generally accepted. Recent knowledge of the anatomical and functional links between brain and body point in a different direction. Brain researchers now believe that what happens in the body can affect the brain, and what happens in the brain can affect the body. Hope, purpose, and determination are not merely mental states. They have electrochemical connections that play a large part in the workings of the immune system and, indeed, in the entire economy of the total human organism.

— Norman Cousins, *Head First: The Biology of Hope*

Activity

One of the best approaches is to observe yourself, your family, your colleagues, and your students over time, keeping a record based on the following questions:

1. **Has bad health ever "got you down"? Has it ever dulled or affected**

   - Your capacity to work?
   - Your capacity to pay attention?
   - Your motivation and interest?
   - Your awareness and enjoyment?

2. **Do there seem to be some correlations in your experience between stressful and unhappy events in your life and bad health? For example:**

   - Colds or flu, perhaps on a regular basis, after the semester ends?
   - Eye strain or backache associated with a particular place, person, or event?
   - Burnout?
   - Ill health following difficulties with personal relationships?

3. **Have your health, capacity, and performance ever improved after**

- Changing your diet?

- Beginning to exercise more?

- Finding a happier relationship?

- Moving to a community where you feel at home?

- Using relaxation exercises on a regular basis?

- Having insight into a problem so that it no longer bothers you?

4. **Do the above relate to what happens in schools? How?**

- What happens to students under time pressures unrelated to learning?

- How many things are scheduled for "convenience" (bus schedules, lunches, assemblies) rather than out of respect for children's (and adults') physical rhythms?

- What happens in class when children or young adults don't get enough sleep? (We can tell you that their ability to absorb new memories is impaired for 48 hours after one night's bad sleep.)

- What happens when, on a daily basis, we induce continuous anxiety in students by means of time pressure, inconsistent rules, and essentially meaningless activities?

- What does a twenty-minute rush to lunch do to the digestive system?

Commentary

All the physiological factors that influence health and well-being influence learning. These factors work in many different ways. Here are three.

1. Poor diet and lack of sleep and exercise all contribute to stress, and one frequent consequence of stress is poor self-esteem. Low self-esteem, we also know, sets limits on what we believe we are capable of learning.

Notes

2. Diet may be implicated in both low activity and hyperactivity.

3. Drug use and abuse can severely restrict the capacity to pay attention and interfere with positive social relationships.

The point to remember is that all our physical systems perform a delicate balancing act and that they are easily "bent out of shape." Our picture of the best learner and best teacher therefore deals with balance. The best societies, families, and schools provide a positive, supportive, health-conscious environment in which individuals can experience the most of life and learning. We should add that we are talking here of wellness, and it goes far beyond what we now generally mean by wellness, which is "not sick."

Physiology and the Construction of Natural Knowledge

All the systems of the body/mind are involved in the learning of those categories and procedures that shape the self, which includes anything that becomes part of our natural knowledge. An example is the way we learn about greetings in real life.

For children in certain cultures, when the ritual of shaking hands or doing a "high five" is established,

The entire body, including muscles and posture, is involved.

A set of specific hand and arm movements is used.

There is eye-to-eye contact or at least some use of the eyes.

There is ongoing use of language.

There are many other sounds besides language.

We have feelings, varying from feeling anxious and threatened to being challenged. All of our senses contribute to the perception of the global context.

Activity

Select for examination an idea, behavior, or influence that seems to be very important to one of your students. Anything that involves peer group pressure is a good example. Simply look for as many components as you can find that contribute to its existence.

Here are some questions to guide you in learning about the observed behavior:

What sorts of words are used when discussing the idea or behavior?

Whose grammar is used?

What tones of voice are used?

What obvious emotions are expressed?

What movements toward or away from people are made?

How does the speaker use body space?

In what ways does clothing change or remain the same?

What attitudes toward others—with respect to sex, age, position in the community, nationality, income level, and so on— are expressed?

What music is favored?

What sort of eye contact is made?

Is there any touching? Of what kind?

What food tends to be eaten? When and where?

As these and other questions come to mind, ask yourself:

What is this person actually learning that is shaping the self?

What role is his or her physiology playing?

Commentary

You are observing natural knowledge being formed through the complex interaction of every physiological and mental system that a person has. Much more is happening than a multisensory presentation of one very simple idea. The way that the systems move in real life has an enormous impact. For example, the notion of "mother" or "father" emerges through a wide range of experiences over time. Any concept that is properly learned is learned in the same way. Another way to test the ways in which natural knowledge is formed is to observe the rhythm and nature of the way different people speak. Are some dull and others dramatic and emotional? Do some use their hands more than others? These are further examples of the fact that meaningful learning requires the entire body and is "stored" in the body. Body language is an example of the fact that our ideas and attitudes actually shape and are also shaped by the ways in which we use our bodies.

Implications for Teaching

One of the drawbacks of traditional teaching is that we tend to separate sensory input and health from language or learning. The practical consequence is that we dilute messages and often remove much of the meaningfulness from course content. The fact is that a full range of physiological and sensory processes operates in every student in every classroom. These processes are involved in multiple ways in every message that you and your students send and receive. They need to be integrated and orchestrated so that they operate in support of each other. When that happens, course content is on its way to becoming natural knowledge.

Note that we are talking of more than just repeating one single message using two or three different senses (such as word, chalkboard, and touch). Oversimplification of sensory modalities, such as an overreliance on simple distinctions between visual, auditory, and kinesthetic learning styles, interferes with creation of the richly textured experiences that learners actually need.

One solution is to assist students in enhancing their sensory acuity and increase the use of all their senses so that their perceptions are richer, more detailed, and more interesting. We have included several exercises in the chapters on principle four and elsewhere for that purpose.

Health also plays a very important role. Healthy systems operate better than unhealthy ones. They tend to absorb information more efficiently and respond in more balanced ways. Mind, body, and health are inter-connected. Hence the way we treat students will sig-nificantly affect whether they are ill or healthy, unhappy or happy. Understanding and appreciating this inter-relationship is essential to our capacity to orchestrate the learning environment and their experiences.

Interactions are complex. Thus posture and breathing influence vision and hearing. We will see in later chapters that education must be built around complex experiences, involving real projects, stories, and so on. One reason for so organizing education is that such activities require students to use their bodies in the complex ways that are essential for real meaningfulness to be experienced.

Here are some questions to guide you:

- To what extent are feelings and emotions such as joy, empowerment, and contentment generated within the school context?

- How is helplessness fostered in the classroom? In the school?

- What might the physiological consequences of fostering helplessness be?

- How are personal rhythms and need for quiet and/or excitement fostered?

- How much of student time in the classroom is spent in activities that use the physical senses and movement?

All mental processes, including learning, are substantially influenced by our physiology.

Notes

Inner and outer reflect each other

8

Principle Three

The Search for Meaning Is Innate

We have established that our brains are engaged in multiple, simultaneous processes every waking minute and that we can focus on one particular event even while the brain is organizing events in holistic records and memories. Principle Three reveals in more depth how the brain goes about actively organizing incoming information in order to make sense of life experience.

If we refer to the ways in which we use and learn about formal greetings, we find that more is needed than just a complex experience. In either an articulated or unarticulated way, we are also asking such questions as

Do I like this person?

What's this all about?

What happens next?

This feels strange, doesn't it?

These questions are real, and they provide a focus—a seed—around which meanings form. Those meanings will relate somehow to our previous experiences, thoughts, and feelings. The brain searches for these linkages continually. The brain needs and automatically registers the familiar while simultaneously searching for and responding to novel stimuli. In effect, we are biologically programmed to make sense of our experience. In other words, we are innately motivated to search for meaning.

The search for meaning occurs at many levels. For example, we need to understand how to move around in our physical world, how to avoid accidents, how to find nourishment, and so on. Beyond these situations, we need to grasp the significance of gestures, words, actions, and the like so that we can build effective relationships. At more sophisticated levels is the need to master the more complex ideas, images, and symbols that explain why things are the way they are, how and why cultures are different, and all the subtle and hidden agendas and meanings that infuse life.

The following activities will allow us to monitor the ways the brain begins its search for meaning, how the different ways feel, and how content can be meaningful in a variety of ways. (There are no right or wrong answers).

Exploring Your Personal World

Activity

Take some time to observe the ways in which young children explore their worlds. Watch them crawl, touch, move, taste, and seek attention. What do you think they are trying to do? In what way are these actions a search for meaning?

Then watch as adolescents imitate each other, model celebrities, adapt their dress and behavior to the expectations of peers, and engage in activities that are deeply absorbing. What do you think they are trying to do? In what ways are these actions a search for meaning?

Finally, identify a setting in which you know you might feel a little strange and out of place. Examples could include an industrial complex, an ethnic community, a cinema that features movies that you do not tend to see. Observe the ways in which you

- look for landmarks and indicators that help you get a sense of where you are;

- react to dress and behavior codes that might be different from yours;

- compare where you are and what you see with the people and places that you find familiar

In what ways are these actions a search for meaning?

Commentary

Much of what drives people in a new context is the need to make sense of it. This need causes people to engage in activities ranging from developing spatial maps so that we can navigate (as in finding our way out of a large parking lot) to assessing and evaluating behaviors that are either comforting or threatening. All of these activities are survival based. And all students are engaging in this process during their years in school. Sometimes they make instant judgments. There is a tendency to make these judgments when they are downshifted or feel relatively helpless. But behind almost all behavior is a set of decisions people have made as to what makes sense for them. When people do not pay attention in class, for instance, they have usually decided that paying attention is essentially meaningless. Our job is to appreciate and then to capitalize on this never-ending search for meaning.

Exploring the Search for Meaning in an Instructional Setting

Activity

In a relaxed and safe environment, close your eyes, relax, and watch the activities of your mind when you consider the following statement:

"We will learn something about the Hopi Indians."

Spend several minutes considering the topic. Just be watchful of your thoughts and feelings. Then record your impressions as they relate to the questions below. If you are in a group, conduct the exercise individually and then discuss as a group.

What images or thoughts occurred when you considered the topic?

To what degree were your previous or current experiences reflected in your thoughts?

Can you identify particular attitudes or emotions you felt? Which ones?

Commentary

Our brains search for experiences that relate to topics or to the context. Before we even begin to learn, our brains are preparing or anticipating in some way. This preparation may include both positive and negative memories and expectations. We may react to this mental preparation with anxiety, indifference, anticipation, or some other state. It is important that we, as teachers and instructors, be aware of this tendency of the brain to ready itself for learning. Processing the experiences, attitudes, feelings, dispositions, and expectations is important in helping the individual and the group organize content effectively.

Activity

You are informed,

> **"The Hopi view themselves as a part of the natural events in life. Even ordinary events become opportunities for celebration."**

Imagine that this idea really appealed to you and that you suddenly realized that by learning about the Hopis we might be able to learn how to make small events in our lives more significant and how our busy lives can be less fragmented and more successful.

What new and different images and feelings occur?

What questions come to mind that would be important to you?

If your thoughts and feelings changed from your initial impressions, why do you think they changed?

Commentary

The brain's search for meaning is very personal. The greater the extent to which what we learn is tied to our personal lives, to our lived experience, the greater the response will be. As you become ready to understand how specific content can relate to your daily experience, note how the activity of your brain increases. More images, perhaps greater anticipation, perhaps specific situations in your life are now apparent in your mind. In essence, the brain has already begun the ordering process of assimilating meaning.

The more teachers and instructors can build bridges between content and human experience, the more meaningful and effective the learning experience will be. We can learn to see that all content has various levels of meaning.

Activity

Compare your reactions as the information below is developed with successive attention to "larger" purposes.

"The Hopi Indians sing songs about planting corn and reenact the planting through dance. They view themselves as part of the planting process and as a part of all natural occurrences."

Notes

"Just as the Hopi celebrate this event through ritual, we celebrate significant events such as the Fourth of July through songs, parades, and fireworks. We reflect on the meaning of democracy in our lives and may feel a sense of joy and participation."

Activity

Try to visualize instructional approaches that might be used to enhance each statement.

Ongoing activity

Take a mundane experience and plan some simple rituals to celebrate it as a part of life. As a group, write down your reactions and think about what it would be like to celebrate life through our daily living. Follow this celebration for a week and note your impressions, using this workbook as a daily journal.

A Daily Journal

Notes

Commentary

As the brain processes experience, it always searches for connections. The extent to which we are transformed by these experiences is the extent to which they are meaningful to us. The activities above require us to assimilate meaning at a number of levels. Each of us will come away with our own kind of knowledge, depending on the impact of the information, example, and experiences. For instance, some may well have thought that celebrating a trivial or mundane act for a week was useless or ridiculous. No connections may have been made with formalized celebrations such as holidays. Others might begin to feel that all of life can be viewed as an ongoing celebration. Yet others may have discovered a different way of experiencing the ordinary events of life.

For all perspectives, however, the initial information that Hopis celebrate their participation in the natural events of life may have more specific meaning now, either by contrast or by association. While you may forget specific information, it is unlikely that you will forget experience as easily.

Implications for Teaching

The brain naturally searches for meaning in experience, and every moment of a student's class and school life is an experience that is being interpreted. For content to be mastered appropriately, it must be taught for meaningfulness. For learning to be meaningful, it must be tied to a student's experience. As a corollary, there are two essential ingredients of brain-based learning.

One is to immerse the learner in multiple, complex interactive experiences. We call that orchestrated immersion. The other is active processing. It is the "consolidation and internalization of information, by the learner, in a way that is both personally meaningful and conceptually coherent" (Caine and Caine 1994, 147). In other words, we take advantage of learners' innate drive to make sense by creating appropriate experiences and then by helping them to process those experiences in many more ways. This is how we can facilitate, and to some extent give direction to, the generation of a student's new natural knowledge.

One way to go about enhancing experience and the value of experiences is to have a checklist of questions that assist us in planning and designing educational programs. Here are some sample questions. You might like to develop others for yourself.

Checklist of Questions

✔ Do I provide examples and ask questions that specifically relate to the experience of my students whenever I teach?

✔ Do I create experiences, activities, or simulations from which students can process content and/or skills?

✔ Do I pose problems to which students can apply information and knowledge? Do these problems engage students' imaginations?

✔ Do I provide opportunities for students to share their own meanings and interpretations?

✔ Do I encourage students to build metaphors relating what they are learning to what they already know?

✔ Do I offer creative or practical, service-oriented projects in which students may get involved in active learning?

Notes

Order is present everywhere

9

Principle Four

The Search for Meaning Occurs through Patterning

Meaningfulness involves a sense of connectedness. Ideas, events, feelings, impressions come together as a whole or a series of wholes. Technically we could call these *gestalts*. In effect, they are patterns. Natural knowledge consists of very rich patterns, of connections at multiple levels.

Of course, these patterns involve the experiences, predispositions, and prior knowledge of the person. Hence the patterns are unique, which is why we must give students space to come to their own understandings in their own ways, even if some of the actual outcomes are specified. It may be important for every student to understand what an equation in math is. But every student will personalize that understanding in a unique way.

Perceiving Connections

Activity

Try to learn the following abstract symbols as quickly as you can. As you learn them, monitor what you are doing to learn them.

Note the ways in which you approach learning the symbols.

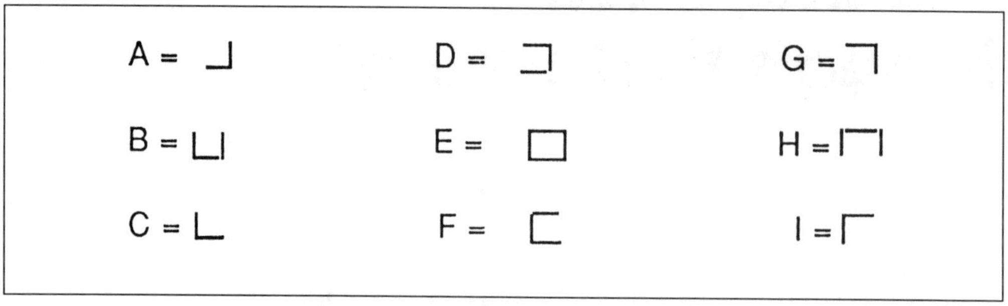

Commentary

When we encounter fragments of information, the brain will seek to establish some kind of pattern, association, or systematic approach. Even if a task is essentially meaningless, we use meaningful patterning procedures to accomplish it.

Activity

Observe the diagram on page 103 and note the ease with which you can now grasp and recall the same symbols.

Obviously, however, there is much more to patterning than this. As a minimum, students need to have some interest or purpose in recalling the symbols; otherwise we are just engaging in sleight of hand and trickery to help them acquire surface knowledge. It is simply sophisticated rote memory. The important aspects of patterning are being ignored. In many respects, of course, this is still just superficial memory. The symbols themselves need to be related to some purpose or interest in order to acquire intrinsic meaning for the student. Some children, for example, may use the symbols as a code for writing "secret" letters.

Commentary

It is imperative that we give students the opportunity to organize content. We must assist them with their patterning. Not only do we remember more quickly when we perceive the world through patterns, but we also retain the information longer. For example, the pattern above can lead to accelerated recall of the abstract symbols.

This exercise involved a highly structured pattern that we have selected. At some level, we may recognize the pattern as the familiar Tic, Tac, Toe symbol. It has meaning in itself. We may even remember childhood experiences in which we played the game, including the emotions, laughter, or personalities involved. Indeed, we may all have some of these childhood experiences, and yet they are different for each one of us. The same process of patterning is still unique. Hence each aspect has some significance for us and can serve to enhance the general meaningfulness of the learning experience.

A	B	C
D	E	F
G	H	I

Recognizing and Creating Patterns

We are born with a set of basic natural categories or patterns that reflect the way the world is. Examples are up and down, light and dark, and lines and edges. We also have a repertoire of other patterns that form quickly and easily, such as the capacity of an infant to recognize faces. Over time richer and richer clusters of patterns take shape in our minds.

One way to describe the patterning process is to say that we look at the world as both scientist and artist. As scientists, we are observers and we seek to explain or understand what we experience. As artists, we are continually acting upon our world expressively. Many times this expression is not apparent, but our choices, priorities, actions, and communication are a part of this expressive process.

Try some conscious patterning processes for yourself.

Activity

Naturally Occurring Patterns

Here are five patterns that occur frequently in nature. They are

> **hexagons**
> **branches**
> **meanderings**
> **spirals**
> **explosions**

You will see these patterns repeated in many ways in the illustrations in this book. Take some time to look for them in your environment.

They are also metaphorical. For instance the plot of a story may branch out, and a character in a novel can explode with passion. Identify some of the metaphorical uses of these patterns in everyday life and in the curriculum.

Patterns in Art

The same patterns are used everywhere in works of art. The artist gives expression to an idea or insight by creating a new pattern that simultaneously uses patterns that are evident in life. Examine the way in which this has been done in the illustration that follows.

The Curriculum as a Set of Patterns

Every subject is a way of organizing life experience in some way. The subjects that we teach and learn are real—they are embedded in the real world. History organizes people and events in places over time. Science deals in part with naturally occurring processes and reactions, from photosynthesis to chemical bonding. A group of people in a meeting hall may also be a political party. Mathematics is a symbolic representation of how much of nature is organized. Thus a line of telegraph poles may be represented by a series, and calculus can be used to deal with the rate of flow of liquids.

When children study a subject that goes beyond their ordinary categories of people, places, and things, they have to perceive and understand a new pattern.

Here are some common patterns that we require students to grasp:

The law of supply and demand

A simple equation

The themes being explored in Hamlet

How immigration shaped the United States

The relative influence of the member nations of the United Nations

Democracy

Ecosystems

These are not just facts. They represent information that has to be put together in patterns that make personal sense to students. Our task is to facilitate the making of those patterns.

For example: What differences would you expect in the insights of students who learn about

democracy in a democratic versus an authoritarian environment?

plant growth from a textbook versus having a garden of their own?

economics from a lecture versus running a small business?

mathematics from a textbook versus devising calculations to be used in laying a sprinkler system or building a tool shed?

Activity

Select one aspect of your curriculum. Look for ways in which the elements that you are teaching can be fully embedded in some real-life experiences available to your students.

Commentary

You will see that experience itself has an organizing power. In fact, it is likely to force you to rearrange the way in which you might otherwise have developed the material you are teaching. Part of our job is to embed material in experiences so that natural patterns can emerge. We will elaborate on this embedding process further, particularly when we address Principle Ten.

Selective Input of Information

The patterns that we perceive depend to a large extent on how we react to the information that is out there. Meaningful learning is not simply a matter of piling up building blocks. The world of experience comes to us in a blitz of patterns. The brain is constantly organizing and making sense of these patterns.

Students tend to be unaware of the input that actually shapes their thinking and perception. Part of our task is to develop increasing awareness of what is actually "out there." Here are some activities for doing that.

Activity

Initial Observation

Look around you. Take a few moments to observe where you are, what you see, what you hear, what is happening.

Just take in the present moment. Briefly describe the experience.

On further observation, what stood out? What did you ignore?

Commentary

If you do this activity with a group, compare your perceptions. The randomness of our perceptions and the different ways we order those perceptions should be evident. One way to test whether they are different is to explore what the scene reminds each of you of. It may also be revealing that some of us are not consciously aware of ourselves as part of our "objective" world. Yet the way we see things, what we see, their impact, and so on are all part of the patterns that drive us in our lives.

Sensory Enhancement

Bertrand Russell, the great British philosopher and mathematician, used to encourage his students to see nature in very great detail. One of the keys to grasping a subject or skill is to be able to perceive it really well in more and more sensory detail, which is why good athletes and musicians pay much attention to the people they select as role models.

The following procedures can help you enhance your sensory awareness, which is also critical to memory and the capacity to focus.

Using gentle sensory deprivation activities to build sensory awareness. The objective of these activities is to reduce some of our sensory input, one sense at a time. Remember that there is no need to be severely discomforted. The exercises can be stopped, or a person can withdraw, at any time. If you do withdraw, however, do not interfere with the experience that others are having. The key is to reflect on and learn something from the entire experience.

In each case, do the activity, and then discuss the answers
to the following review questions:

**Did you feel different in any way? In particular, was there any type of
deprivation that led to genuine discomfort?**

Did the quality of other sensory information change?

**Did your understanding of, and ability to deal with, the messages you
received change?**

**Did you grasp anything about the nature of social relationships or the
way in which groups work?**

Lights out

Sometime during a discussion in your group, turn off the
lights and make the room as dark as you can. Then
continue the discussion.

Blind walk

Divide into pairs. One member of each pair is blindfolded.
The other then leads the blindfolded person through a
room or outside, taking extreme care to help and guide
the person so that any obstacles are overcome safely.
After, say, five to ten minutes, change roles. Note that
someone ought to stay uninvolved to supervise the entire
exercise. Do NOT do anything dangerous.

Turn down the volume

Watch TV without the sound on. Can you understand
what is happening? What do you think about what is
happening? Are there some programs that are better to
watch that way?

Unseen scene

You can experiment with reduced vision in many ways.
For example, you could have a friend drive you to a place
that you want to go to and have never visited, and go
through it with eyes closed or a blindfold on, perhaps
relying on your friend for a description.

Noise and music

Collect a set of tapes of widely differing types of music. Rent a few videos. At those times when the movie you rented relies on background music, turn down the volume and play music of your own choice. Vary it a great deal. How does your response to the movie change?

Note, incidentally, that you are now actively interacting with the movie and not just responding differently. Does your sense of the movie change at all? How would you describe the quality of the experience that you are having? Is doing this activity alone different from doing it with others?

Body listening

Pretend that you really do not like someone who is talking. Exaggerate a body stance to show them what you think (for example, fold your arms and turn away). Have them go on talking, and observe what you hear and what you think about the person, the content of what he or she is saying, and this exercise.

Change positions. Imagine that the other person has become the key to your success and you like him or her **very** much. Lean forward and turn toward the person as he or she talks. Have the person go on talking, and observe what you hear, what you think about the person, the content of what he or she is saying, and this exercise.

Adopt the slouch of pure boredom, sinking into your chair and maybe closing your eyes. Have the person go on talking, and observe what you hear and what you think about the person, the content of what he or she is saying, and this exercise.

Personal space, near and far

During a conversation with someone, alternate between moving in very close to him or her and moving quite far away. Does distance affect the quality of the conversation in any way? Are there differences in preferences between you and your friends? Do some people like to touch or be touched during conversation? Discuss your responses to being touched.

Great taste

Invite some people to prepare one or two delicious desserts or meals and bring them to the group. Experiment with the impact of the aroma on the group. Perhaps one dish could be opened during a meeting. Does it affect interest and attention in any way?

Go out and look for scents that remind you of your youth—perhaps a flower, a particular meal, a place. What memories does the scent bring back to you?

Discuss the perfumes and colognes that people in your group use. What reasons do people give for wearing them or for their reactions to others' scents? What images and beliefs accompany the perfumes?

Using Active Description to Enhance Sensory Awareness

For many reasons, people tend to gloss over what they are experiencing. They just do not perceive the detail that is there. This is a tremendous barrier to effective learning, in part because much of the relevant information is embedded in sensory detail.

Activity

Step 1 Select any ordinary object. A pencil, a car, a computer, a ring will do.

Step 2 Begin to describe the object out loud, in as much detail as possible. You can move it, touch it, walk around it, and so on. Take two to three minutes.

Step 3 Now ask yourself specific sense-based questions that need answers. For example,

> Precisely how long, wide, deep is it?
> What shapes and angles does it have?
> Does it feel rough, smooth, uneven?
> What colors are in or on it?
> Does it hum, shrill, groan, creak?
> Does it have any odor? What?

Take five to seven minutes. Write your responses in the following space.

Step 4 Find a poem, play, or story that you really like. Examine in some depth the way in which the author uses powerful and evocative language to capture the sensory details and qualities of an event, scene, or experience. How important is that aspect of the work for your understanding and appreciation?

Commentary

One of the reasons for introducing great literature and art into the teaching of any subject is that it brings the subject to life, in part by generating sensory and emotional reality.

Using Contemplative Observation to Enhance Sensory Awareness

This exercise follows those used above. In addition you might like to return to it after exploring the meditation and focusing exercises described below.

Activity

Step 1 Take a few deep breaths and relax. Then simply look at the object selected in the exercise above for any period from a few seconds to a few minutes. Do not analyze. Simply allow yourself to observe, and be aware of any additional details or new patterns that come to mind.

Sometimes it helps to see it from another point of view, such as the view of an interior decorator, an artist, an engineer, a parent.

Step 2 Discuss with others what you saw. Reflect on the nature of the experience.

Sample Questions

Did you begin to see more at any point?

Which process revealed most to you?

Were there periods of new information and periods of nothing new?

How did you feel at different stages? Were you interested, bored, agitated, excited, patient, and so on?

How did your feelings color your experience and your observations?

Did any new perception lead to a change in feelings and attitude? Which perception?

Step 3 Repeat this process in different contexts. Here are some suggestions for your observation.

- A scene from nature, such as a park or garden
- A scene in any part of a city
- A masterful performance of an athlete or musician on TV
- A science experiment in a laboratory
- As a professional doctor, sales representative, lawyer, actor, chef

Implications for Teaching

The essence of meaningful learning is the perception and generation, by the student, of patterns that make sense. Our task as educators is to introduce into all that we do the opportunity for students to engage in that patterning. In part we need to build lessons and design classrooms around preselected patterns. These patterns need to be fluid, open-ended, complex, and yet manageable. That is why stories, themes, metaphors, ongoing real projects, and social structures, such as student government, are so important.

We also need to create the sense of freedom and an atmosphere that encourages students to search for and create unique patterns. Using art and music and having students learn about art and music are practical ways to accomplish this sense of freedom. The general thrust must be to embed in the classroom a sense of purpose and multiple expressions of a sense of dynamic wholeness.

As a practical matter, we can begin by keeping in mind questions that guide us in ways of thinking about patterns and about curriculum and instruction.

1. In what ways do I create a learning context in which the search for patterns is an ongoing challenge and expectation?

2. In what ways do I allow students to explore examples and nonexamples in order to derive their own sense of consonance and dissonance?

3. How do I try to seek out and convey "threads" or "themes" that may be inherent in different subjects being studied?

4. How do I use an interdisciplinary approach to teaching at times, so that I go beyond the boundaries of single subjects?

5. Do I ask my students about the related personal experiences that the learning of particular content evokes in them?

6. How do I create multiple approaches to teaching the same thing to illustrate that many options are available in the ways we learn and the insights we perceive?

7. How do I create an environment in which students may discover patterns and meanings for themselves or through interaction with others rather than "telling" them what the patterns are?

Reality consists of matter, energy, and meaning

10

Principle Five

Emotions Are Critical to Patterning

It used to be assumed that concepts and emotion could be totally separated. That is simply wrong. Emotion and cognition interact and energize and shape each other. It is useful and appropriate, at times, to speak of them separately, but they are inseparable in the brains and experiences of learners.

Experiences that involve interactions with others powerfully influence our thinking and reactions. Having or not having significant others, support, bonding, pleasure, confrontation, security, and risk has a major impact on the way that we pattern. For example, we now know that language develops through social interaction. Not only the words, grammar, and style of language, but also our concepts and the values that we express in language are shaped in part by our cultural and emotional experiences and context. In part, that is why we can say that the brain is a social brain.

We need to go far beyond the traditional view that students need to be supported and feel safe. We must grasp the profound interaction of cognition and emotion at many levels, including the level of meaning and concept.

That is why teaching for the expansion of natural knowledge is different from teaching for surface knowledge. Natural knowledge is acquired when students get a "feeling" for the meaning of an idea and when their learning is organized around what the students themselves regard as deeply important.

Attitudes and Values

As we recall patterns of events from our experience, we realize that the events are laden with emotions and feelings.

Activity

Some recollections

Recall some of the following occasions and note your feelings and emotions as you recount the details of that experience:

A holiday, perhaps in your youth, when there was laughter, warmth, and love

A sad occasion in your life that left you overwrought

A time when you felt victorious

A special romantic occasion in your life

Commentary

Emotions influence the intensity and vividness of our memories. Emotions also shape and color our memories. Physical reactions also accompany these memories. There may be smiles, frowns, tears, tension, or increased pulse rate. As we saw in the first two principles, our bodies react physically and emotionally to experience and even to thoughts of experience.

Now repeat this activity, recalling subjects and skills that you might have studied. Examples include

art

math

literature

computing

biology

history

You will see that, at a very basic level, our attitudes about what we studied are highly emotional. Thus, we might learn to draw but dislike drawing, while we struggle through adversity to master math because we find the process exciting. Our challenge, therefore, is to enliven positive emotional attitudes in students both to education generally and to the specifics of the curriculum.

Ideas and Concepts Are Shaped by Emotions and Values

Many of our ideas and beliefs are shaped by the emotional tenor of the way in which we experienced them. We can test this theory by examining some of our notions, such as the ideas of "holiday," "youth," "responsibility," and "freedom." When we look inward, we find that our full understanding of each concept includes a fairly complex emotional color that each engenders in us.

Activity

Read the following selection with a pen or pencil in hand. As you encounter a word that creates an image or a remembrance in your mind, write down your thoughts. Compare your list of images with those of others in your group.

The stars are still shining in the sky as I crawl out of my tent. I feel the morning in the glimmer of the fading moon. My hands rub together almost instinctively, trying to generate some warmth. Why do mornings like this always seem out of the ordinary? Building a fire, I wait impatiently for my first cup of coffee. Finally, the gurgling noise begins that signals the end of a short eternity. Amidst the quiet morning sounds I pour my first cup. I sit back, look at the waking world around me, warm my hands almost sensuously around the cup, and drink my first taste. The morning is perfect.

Commentary

What we often think is an ordinary experience—reading a paragraph—is full of personally constructed images. In some cases, our minds wander to an array of related images that dance from one event to another. These images are patterns of experience by which we construct meaning. Teachers and instructors who recognize that all learning is laden with constructed patterns and meaning can begin to take advantage of this realization, both to enrich and to accelerate the learning experience. Symbols as patterns are full of emotional energy.

When we see teaching as no more than getting information into a student, we miss the richness with which the human brain deals with reality and overlook the much broader spectrum of information that is "there." A fundamental and devastatingly counterproductive consequence is that students can "master" a subject as reflected in test scores and yet be both demotivated from pursuing that subject and largely unaware of what a subject is really all about.

Activity

For one complete day, use your journal to record your emotional responses to different events (such as the news) and messages (such as administrative requirements). Explore the extent to which your understanding of the event or message depended on, was inhibited by, or was shaped by your emotional response.

Activity

Read the phrases below. Note the emotion or situation you believe is expressed in each phrase. Then describe the literal meaning of the phrase.

Emotional Description	Literal Description
Hot under the collar	
Blowing off steam	
Sweet as honey	
I thought I would die	

Commentary

These phrases are obvious metaphors that create images from which we extract certain meanings. Current studies suggest that much of our language involves the unconscious use of metaphors that serve to create patterns of emotional experience. Lakoff and Johnson (*Metaphors We Live By,* 1980) give many examples of this metaphorical use of language. For instance, we think of time as a commodity—we "budget" time, "save" it, "run out of" it, "manage" it, "lose" it, or "waste" it. We see arguments often in terms of war: we "win" arguments, "lose" them, "defend" positions. Each of these metaphorical constructs is deeply emotional. Thus concept and emotion are linked.

We Impose Old Patterns on New Experience

As we develop our worldview, contoured and colored by emotions and values and expectations, we naturally interpret new experiences in terms of patterns that are already established. Thus, we tend to think of a new shopping mall in terms of how we feel about malls. Students, similarly, may face a new year of math with the mindset they acquired at an earlier time. Bigotry and prejudice are extreme examples of these closed patterns. In *Mindfulness,* Ellen Langer calls these fixed patterns "category traps." We all have them, and they act as barriers to new learning.

Activity

Note and discuss some opinions that you have held for many years. Reflect on how strongly you hold them. Ask yourself, "What sort of evidence and experience would it take to change my mind?" Some possible examples follow:

Political beliefs

Opinions of different cultural practices

Your ability to excel at a particular sport, playing the piano, financial investments, time management, learning another language, math, relationships, or in some other area

According to Langer (1989), "Mindlessness is the rigid reliance on old categories, mindfulness means the continual creation of new ones" (63). Thus, a central aspect of the work of educators is to engender a capacity for "active uncertainty" in students and in ourselves. This uncertainty includes the ability to accept uncertainty, tolerate ambiguity, and welcome new insights.

Activity

This activity can take as little as a few minutes and as long as a lifetime. Simply select one idea or concept that you feel fairly confident about. Then ask yourself two questions:

1. **What else is there to learn about this?**

2. **How else could I go about finding new insights on this topic?**

We invite you to answer these questions briefly now, using the space below to make notes. *Note:* You could do this in even more depth by first practicing one of the relaxation activities that we describe in appendix C.

Implications for Teaching

We have seen that the brain is patterning all the time. The additional insight is that patterns of understanding are intrinsically emotional. The emotional "color" of a concept is actually part of its meaning.

The result is that we need to create an intelligent emotional climate in which to embed every subject we teach. Students' understanding is affected by the nature of their interpersonal relationships, by the emotional qualities of the particular examples and metaphors that are selected, by the hidden themes and agendas in which content is embedded, and so on.

Ultimately, students must acquire a "feel" for a subject in order to genuinely understand it. In *Making Connections* we therefore talk about "felt meaning." That inner sense and relationship are characteristic of the relationship that experts have with their fields of expertise. We must work with that "feel" from the very beginning.

We can now see that incorporating a full range of emotions into content in appropriate ways is absolutely essential for the construction and generation of natural knowledge by students.

Here are some questions to serve as guides.

1. **Do I create an environment that values what students think about learning generally and content specifically?**

2. **Do I create a supportive setting that allows students to question, make mistakes, and try out ideas?**

3. **Do I honor students' contributions in a way that encourages their involvement?**

4. **Do I have a focus on what students "feel" when they are learning and what relevance or nonrelevance the learning of particular material has for their lives?**

5. Do I help students establish a purpose for learning what I am teaching that somehow relates to their lives and experience?

6. Do I look for underlying themes in the material I teach that relate in any way to life's "big questions"?

7. Do I approach learning as being both rigorous and joyous?

8. Do I create opportunities for mastery and performance that build pride into what is learned?

9. Do I create with students applications for learning that are practical and make a difference somewhere?

10. Do I make learning a social encounter as well as an individual one?

Everything is both part and whole simultaneously

11

Principle Six

Every Brain Simultaneously Perceives and Creates Parts and Wholes

The brain builds relationships and wants to see how things "fit" or connect. It does this through two separate but simultaneous tendencies for organizing information. One is to reduce information to parts. The other is to perceive and work with information as a whole or series of wholes. These two tendencies are actually the main discovery of the left brain/right brain research.

The brain is designed to perceive interconnectedness. Thus, we perceive the whole puzzle even though we are focusing our attention on only one individual piece, and conversely, we can look at the entire puzzle and see the individual pieces embedded in it.

This process is actually quite complex. But of course, it is what makes integration of content areas and life experience so important in education. In fact, every subject deeply interpenetrates every other subject. Each is a part of another subject, and each is a whole of which other subjects are part. We can use history as an example.

Any point in history came as a result of what passed before it and shaped the future, which is now our present. Learning history is never simply a matter of memorizing specific events, dates, and places. History consists of living, thinking, breathing, and feeling people creating a reality.

Notes

The poetry that people of individual cultures compose is forged by their experiences. Their literature reflects their hopes, dreams, disappointments, and physical realities. Their music and songs reflect the joys and pains of human life on earth. Their technology, agriculture, economics, and art are connected in experience.

History must be taught in such a way that we re-create such realities as whole experiences for our learners. Only then can students understand events and decisions and acquire a sense of the deeper linkages.

Examples of Wholes

There are many natural wholes that infuse life. They can all be called upon in education.

Activity

The following exercise is designed to help you realize how intimately everything is connected to a greater reality, how greater realities always contain parts, and that neither can really exist without the other. It is also designed to help you understand that the brain is capable of holding a range of images at the same time and that teaching needs to respect both parts and wholes. We tend to focus on one aspect at a time. Ultimately, however, the parts are unique and are perceived differently when we see them as aspects of a larger or deeper whole. Unfortunately, this wholeness tends to be ignored in education.

Step 1   Begin by playing some relaxing music (perhaps *Comfort Zone* by Steven Halpern or another tape capable of inducing a reflective state). Lean back and take a few deep breaths.

Step 2   Only after completing step 1, read the following to yourself or have someone read it slowly to you (you can experiment and learn from your reactions so that you understand better how to use this method in your teaching).

In the text, each period corresponds to approximately one second. Thus ". . ." would indicate an interval of three seconds. The less experience you have with using imagery, the longer the time should elapse between words.

To experience the principle, engage as many of your senses, and as much of your intellect and emotion, as possible. The richer the experience, the more potential there is for expansion of awareness at deep levels.

Look at one of your hands . . . . . Imagine that you are inside a zoom lens moving ever closer to your hand . . . . . You are now inside the skin . . . . . now inside the cells . . . . . and when you are ready, move to the atoms that make up your hand . . . . . and then to subatomic levels . . . . .

Now reverse this process and slowly move back up from the subatomic level . . . . . to the atoms that make up your hand . . . . to skin and hand . . . and now step back a bit and see your hand as part of your arm . . . . your body . . . . the room you are in . . . . the house . . . . .

Now zoom out to include the neighborhood . . . your state . . . . . the country . . . . the planet . . . . . . the solar system . . . . . and the galaxy . . . . . Now come back step by step to the point where you began.

Step 3   Reflect for a moment on this exercise, using the questions that follow, and record your impressions below.

Jot down any general impressions you may have had. For instance, how "real" was this journey?

How does interconnectedness "feel"? Did you feel it in any specific part of your body? Do you now? What emotions did you experience (positive, negative, or neutral)?

What would you change were you to do the exercise again? Would you do it again? What would you watch for if you were to lead someone else through this exercise?

Step 4   Return for a moment to your reflective state by recalling your experience as clearly as possible. Now explore the following questions:

Which part of the sequence can you eliminate and still experience this hand in this moment in time? The cells? The atoms? Your body? The house? (perhaps you are outdoors?) Would this hand exist without a planet? a solar system? a universe?

What does interconnectedness mean to you? Of what does it remind you? How would you define it? Where do you find it in life?

Is anything not part of the greater whole?

Commentary

Most education focuses on each of the facets of our learning as discrete, independent objects of study, not as events that touch and define each other. However, every experience contains this continuum you just experienced with the journey in and beyond your hand. Every segment we focus on is somehow related and connected to other elements and events. Understanding these connections is not only crucial to learning differently, it is at the heart of the thinking that helps you change the way you teach.

Stories and Projects: Natural Wholes

Stories

One way to begin to create connections is through the medium of storytelling. Children acquire a sense of narrative when they are very young. In part this is a consequence of a particular memory system—the locale memory system dealt with in more depth in chapters 9 and 10. That memory system is largely autobiographical and stores our own life story.

The power and fascination of stories continues through our entire lives. Thus, almost every detailed item in the news is in story form.

Think about it. Early humans developed stories to pass on religious, historical, scientific, and cultural knowledge. Subsequent generations added new versions and developed extensive ways to express the meaning these stories communicated. Probably a majority of our personal communication is telling stories of particular incidents and happenings in our day-to-day lives. During nostalgic times we often recount moments of the saga of our own self-narrative. There is a sense of wholeness, connectedness, and meaning that is conveyed in a story that would otherwise be only irrelevant fragments of experience.

There is a notable difference in the engagement of students (any age) between when a story is told and when facts are simply presented. When the story illustrates a larger truth that can be explored through subsequent activities, it takes on even greater power.

When a story is retold or extended by students through expressive arts such as poetry, drawings, drama, and dance to illustrate the ways in which the story connects to other learnings, the power is enhanced further. The story of "photosynthesis," of a "fraction," of "Hamlet," of "Booker T. Washington," of "division," of "a nation," of "a feeling," of "a concept," and so on, integrates the life of the "character" within the "contexts" and "relationships" of the story line. The narrative of real, fanciful, and even abstract subjects somehow relates to a recognition of our own self-narrative.

Activity

Pool the knowledge of your group to explore the following questions:

What are the basic elements of a story? (for example, characters, setting, plot)

What types of story are there? (for example, thematic story, historical narrative)

In what contexts have you seen stories used effectively? (for example, the news, telling stories to small children, at dinner parties, gossip)

How could you use stories effectively in your learning and teaching?

Projects

A project has a purpose that naturally organizes the attention and efforts of people. It also generates a specific set of questions (for example, How do I measure the area of the roof? Where can I find out how to connect an electric light? What software can I use to create a database?)

Examine some projects in which you have been engaged recently.

How did they organize your time?

What sorts of questions did you ask?

To what extent did you have a sense of your ultimate goal even before you knew how you were going to get there?

Commentary

With both stories and projects, note that we begin with a sense of the whole even though there are many specifics that still need to be worked out. That is how the brain likes to function. It is designed to blend and connect details into larger wholes that make sense.

There is an even larger message. Stories and projects do not come into existence out of nowhere. They are also part of something larger. Sometimes they are part of the ongoing life story and career of an individual. Sometimes they are part of a larger project such as setting up a business. And these are also part of something larger still.

Implications for Teaching

We need to experience the richness of interconnectedness. Everything is embedded in a greater something, and everything has parts within it. That is why really meaningful learning is a matter of discerning what Bateson in *Steps to an Ecology of Mind* (1972) called "the patterns that connect."

The brain is designed to deal with this interplay because the interplay is a part of the interconnectedness. Indeed, when we break content up into fragments we actually make it more difficult for students to learn. Once we introduce life into learning, we gain access to a repertoire of methods and ideas that is unlimited.

We just need to recognize and take advantage of our resources and use wholeness in education.

Here are some vehicles to guide you in combining parts and wholes:

- Multiple use of stories
- Team teaching
- An integrated curriculum
- Global themes
- Large projects
- Ecological thinking of all types

What is, is always in process

12

Principle Seven

Learning Involves Both Focused Attention and Peripheral Perception

Diane Halpern (1989) tells of a conversation she once had with a cab driver. She and the driver had been discussing the way in which laundry products are advertised on television. The cab driver insisted that he never paid any attention to such advertising and that he always just got the blue bottle that got out "ring around the collar." Halpern goes on to say, "Although he believed that he was not allowing the advertising claims to influence him, in fact, they were directly determining his buying habits" (8).

The point of Principle Seven is that the brain is continually scanning the entire context we are in at any moment. Thus, even when we are not directly aware of all that we are sensing, we are nevertheless including in our decisions everything that we are experiencing. The practical implication? Content is never separate from context.

Have you ever experienced a familiar smell that also brought with it a number of sensory and qualitative memories? Every so often I am in a building that smells like the elementary school I attended as a child. The smell also brings with it a hoard of other impressions relating a sense of excitement, loneliness, and other feelings more difficult to label. I am certain that I never consciously thought about these various impressions as my brain was busy registering them.

The entire context you are in at any moment exerts powerful influences over your mood and, what is more important, your brain's biasing mechanisms. As with the cab driver we mentioned, these peripheral signals will influence what you ultimately do—and come to know—regardless of whether you register such information consciously.

Activity

Step 1   For just a moment, think of your favorite restaurant. Now try to "feel" it. Pay particular attention to what makes this place special. Is the food the only thing? What about the ambience? How do the foods and service and setting plus your memories all act together to make this a special place? Are there other impressions that are equally real but that are hard to put into words?

List some of the things that come to mind.

Step 2   Notice how, when we have a choice, we pick the neighborhood in which we choose to live because it seems right or feels right. Notice also that you know immediately when the atmosphere you find yourself in is not what it should be or is one that makes you happy or comfortable.

What are the indirect messages given by your neighborhood? Your home? What do both reflect about you? Your values? How do they influence you in turn? Your expectations?

Commentary

Peripheral stimuli affect how or whether we deal with incoming information. When safety and some sense of comfort are absent, for example, your natural survival mechanisms will become vigilant for potential danger (the signals that tell us we are not safe or comfortable may be extremely subtle or highly personal). We all have this reaction even though different reactions will be triggered by different situations for different individuals. A sense of danger is aggravated by a sense of helplessness and forces our brains and our bodies to revert to accustomed survival behaviors.

The opposite tends to be true as well. When the peripheral messages spell safety and relaxation, we tend to be more open to looking at our experiences in new and more creative ways.

Activity

Step 1   Pay attention to how people "orchestrate" their environments. Large companies are very interesting. The higher an individual's status, the better the furnishings as a rule. Paintings become more elaborate, as does the furniture. Plants are usually present and more visible than those used in work spaces of workers lower in the hierarchy.

Why? Is such decorating done on purpose?

Step 2   Apply these notions to an evaluation of your local school. Keep in mind that children need protection, gentleness, and order in their surroundings. Look at the myriad messages that express what kind of values are held by the adult world students will emulate. Remember that they learn what they experience and that peripheral messages are a powerful part of their experience.

What is the ratio of living plants to concrete on the outside of the building, and what is the ratio of open spaces to closed walls and other enclosures, such as fences?

How is the emotional climate expressed by peripherals? How many negative messages do you see? What positive, uplifting messages do you see?

Are rules constricting or do they refer to cooperation and shared responsibilities?

Are the messages that various teachers send to students contradictory?

How are teacher, school, parental, and community values expressed? Are there mixed messages?

In instruction, is music restricted to music lessons or are musical instruments allowed and encouraged at other appropriate times?

Is real play a part of the learning process?

Do you hear singing in regular classes (both for middle and high schools)?

How is imagination incorporated into the curricula?

Are time schedules constrictive or can students do longer, more involved projects that take two to three hours or days?

What are these children learning about the world? About themselves as learners?

Commentary

We need to recognize that we live and work in complex environments that are rich in signals, messages, and information, much of which is unarticulated and indirect. These messages influence attitudes and states of mind and, therefore, how much we will risk, how relaxed and caring we can be, how self-protective and mean we will be. Once we become sensitive to the environmental messages, we can begin to take charge of the peripheral messages that are being sent.

Renate once gave a talk on stress management in an elementary school cafeteria. Her entire message focused upon creating a relaxed and positive atmosphere. Huge posters on the walls spelled out such messages as, "Say No to drugs." The pictures in the posters were frightening, and these posters were the only things decorating that cafeteria. Yes, we want children to be aware of the destructive force of drugs, but creating fear and stress will not convey the whole message. For children to be happy, safe, protected, and savvy, we have to deal with fearful issues in a context that includes positive messages about life. In short, we need to direct children to how they can experience the fullness of life.

Peripherals are very important because they color our impressions and determine how we will react. Generally speaking, art, classical music, living plants, orderliness in room arrangements, and visual stimuli affect us differently than do disorder, blank walls, or disorganized decorations. Keeping the effect of peripherals in mind when we orchestrate our environments helps us to utilize intelligently this natural tendency of the brain.

Implications for Teaching

> *It's the scientists themselves who give Woods Hole its unmistakable air. Whether waiting for the drawbridge that bisects the town to be lowered or for a bowl of chowder in a local restaurant, they are in constant conversation. Their scientific jargon —"ATP," "calcium spikes," "symbiotic bacteria"— always fills the air, mingling at the beach with the lapping of the waves or in a restaurant with the smells of coffee and fried clams.*
>
> *And it's not just their conversations but also their behavior that distinguishes them from nonscientists. In this town full of observers of nature, everyone makes eye contact with everyone else.*
>
> — Susan Allport, *Explorer of the Black Box*

Peripheral stimuli are operating whether we like it or not. They are part of reality and they contribute to the packaging of every message that a learner receives. They include "light" stimuli—barely perceptible but nevertheless quite potent signals. Hence, they contribute to the formation of natural knowledge.

First, peripheral stimuli influence the atmosphere and climate in which education occurs. We will show later that students and educators both need to be in a state of relaxed alertness for the optimal generation of natural knowledge. Hence the environment must be orchestrated to free ourselves and our students from the influence of signals that inhibit learning. One key here is congruence. An administrator or a teacher who is basically uncaring or incompetent will not change that impression regardless of how many plants are in her office or what kind of classical music he plays.

Second, peripheral signals are part of the content of any message. Natural knowledge is formed on the basis of the entirety of a student's experience. Therefore, reality must be consistent with content.

The following questions may serve as guidelines:

Is your classroom linked with life and nature and in a way that is also orderly?

Do you have appropriate "gentle" rituals and procedures that orient students to your class and to specific tasks?

Does your entire school demonstrate support for the kind of values you treasure?

Is your community involved in supporting school goals and functions? Do these goals include an appreciation of intellectual activities?

Do teachers in your school agree on common rules of courtesy?

All in all, are students in a healthy, intellectually challenging environment?

Are the decorations, building, and grounds of your school conducive to learning and developing mentally and physically healthy citizens?

Does your classroom give students experiences in democratic decision making?

What would your ideal school look like? Where can you begin?

Everything comes in layers

13

Principle Eight

Learning Always Involves Conscious and Unconscious Processes

This principle is closely related to, but actually expands, Principle Seven. That principle refers to complex signals our brains pick up from the environment. For learning to happen, those signals and messages need to be combined, organized, integrated, and transformed. Ultimately, they must *make sense*. We tend to believe that making sense is an active, conscious process. That, however, is only part of the picture. Much of what happens is actually unconscious.

The educator is never in control of the learning. It is the brain that learns. That is its job. Our task is to know about both conscious and unconscious activity and to help each level do its job more effectively. It is through a grasp of design and orchestration that we accomplish this learning.

The Reality of Two Levels of Processing

Activity

Here are some questions to ask yourself and to discuss with others:

Have you ever worked hard on a problem without understanding it, only to find an answer coming to you after you have stopped thinking about the problem?

Have you ever gone to sleep with a problem on your mind and awakened with a solution in the morning?

Have you ever had a traumatic or delightful experience that seems to have an ongoing influence on you even when you are not thinking about it?

Commentary

Each of these experiences is familiar to most of us. The first two are relied on extensively by those who deal in creative problem solving. The "Aha!" of insight that we often have comes quite out of the blue. The reason is that the brain/mind has been working on it below the threshold of awareness. The third—being influenced long after an event has occurred—is right at the heart of psychotherapy. One of the reasons that counseling is so important to many people is that they have "unfinished business"—problems and issues—that goes on influencing them subconsciously.

These aspects of experience turn out to be enormously valuable to educators, because the experiences confirm the operation of subconscious thinking. Once we find better ways to enhance and capitalize on the subconscious, we can teach much more effectively. In fact, that is the reason why the peripherals referred to in Principle Seven are so important. When we use them appropriately, they contribute to effective unconscious processing of information.

Activity

Visibles and Invisibles

Find a leaf or flower or something from nature. Respond to the following two instructions BEFORE proceeding.

Describe in detail what is visible to you—the color, veins, texture, and so on.

Now focus on invisibles. Ask yourself what created this leaf (the tree, roots, nutrients, water, photosynthesis and so on).

The critical questions are

> **What part of the visibles can you remove and still have this object be what it is?**
>
> **What part of the invisibles can you remove and still have it be what it is?**

The answer: None

Commentary

This example relates deeply to Principle Seven. In every visible act or experience are any number of invisible elements that are hidden but that are nevertheless very powerful in affecting what we see or what we experience.

Take another look at your plant. What or who created it?

What or whoever created it also created us. The message is even deeper, however. When we are developing or creating thoughts, much that happens is equally invisible—even to ourselves.

The Role of Consciousness in Problem Solving

Conscious thought is clearly essential to understanding. We must analyze and think about issues and problems. However, the key point is that insight does NOT necessarily occur during the times of conscious analysis.

One of the basic functions of conscious thought is to prime the unconscious mind. In other words, one of our jobs is to facilitate the invisible process. If we use thinking productively, we also help our unconscious to go on thinking effectively.

This process is captured by Mark Helprin (1975):

> *Najime walked every day to the seaside, and stayed there from noon to evening, smoking his pipe and staring at the white foam of the waves and their curling, like his smoke. He knew that an idea of victory could come either deliberately or on the air. But he knew also that ideas of victory which seem to travel on the air alight always on the shoulders of those who have been laboring in thought.*

This approach has been systemized by such experts as Ned Herrmann, who teaches creative problem solving.

Activity

Problem Solving Exercise

You might like to venture straight into experimenting with the technique. You might, as an alternative, discuss the process with colleagues to see if it or something like it ever has worked for any of you. Read through the following steps first, then go back and respond:

Step 1 **Identify a manageable problem in your life that needs an insightful solution.**

Talk it through, discuss it, write it down, express it in different ways

Step 2 **Gather all the information you can.**

Ask questions. Talk to people. Read books. Watch videos. Observe people and events.

Step 3 **Elaborate creatively.**

Find a variety of ways to think about and experience the problem and the information. Go to the top of a tall building and think about perspective. Play with a map of the world and think about interconnectedness. Pretend to be different people involved and think about different points of view.

Step 4 **Incubate.**

Leave the problem alone in your mind for a while, even though doing so can be very difficult. Sometimes you need to get so involved in something else that you actually do not have the time or energy to bother about your problem.

Sometimes it is a matter of simply taking a break—exercise, relax, go to a movie, do some gardening. Sometimes it is a matter of consciously giving yourself permission to think about other things—for an hour, a week, or longer.

In practice, good problem solvers often do return to think about problems more, as in the story from which we quoted, and often in different contexts. It may be in a restaurant, on the beach, at a party, or in some other setting. Feel free to do this sometimes, provided you take some genuine time away from the problem.

Step 5 **"Aha!" solutions emerge.**

Be awake to them. You may have a dream in which an insight is embedded. You may overhear a remark in a conversation that points the way. You may be singing in the shower when an idea comes to mind. You may get lots of insights. Make a point of noting them. Perhaps keep a small notebook with you. Or record your dreams when you wake up.

Note: This "aha" experience is what we have described as "felt meaning." It is the essential aspect of learning that leads to the acquisition of new natural knowledge.

Step 6 **Test your insight.**

This test can be difficult because your idea may be contrary to conventional wisdom. Find ways to try it out in practice and discuss it with people whom you know to have open and questioning minds.

Commentary

Although the process we have described has been used for many years, most people do not relate it to learning in school. In principle, however, much the same thing is happening. To a large extent, meaningful learning is insightful problem solving. As we point out above, these new "felt meanings" constitute the extent to which there is an expansion of natural knowledge.

Students are being inundated with vast amounts of information, and their job is to understand it. That means that it has to make sense, or come together. That is what a creative insight is. In fact, there will be many insights, large and small, some of which will be unnoticed. Some come quickly. Some are a long time in coming. The safest point to remember is that insightful learning takes time.

On many occasions the process does not seem to work. One extremely important reason is that we must actually be open to possibilities and must believe that we have the capacity to achieve our results. That state of mind, which we call relaxed alertness in *Making Connections,* is vital for meaningful learning. It is dealt with in more depth in Principle Eleven.

Activity

Think back on and discuss all the principles we have explored thus far from the point of view of the roles of the conscious and unconscious mind. For example,

1. **Is it possible for your brain to be a parallel processor if all thoughts and operations need to be conscious?**

2. **Is it possible to be consciously aware of every aspect of the physiology that is engaged in learning?**

3. **Is it possible for us to be in control of, or aware of, all the emotions that we experience?**

4. **Do you consciously divide a scene into all the different parts and wholes?**

5. **Can you be aware of all the peripheral signals that are influencing you?**

Notes

Commentary

There is much happening in our brains that we are not and cannot be aware of. We have tended to think of unconscious processes in terms of body maintenance. There is more. Our brains are processing information without our being aware of it, which is actually of enormous value to educators. It means that we have available to us a very powerful resource. It also changes our focus because we do not have to assume that our job is to use the conscious mind exclusively for learning. Rather, we can also use the conscious mind as a way of priming the unconscious mind. In effect, our job is to help the brain do its job.

Active Uncertainty

In order to capitalize upon the power of unconscious processing, we must use our conscious minds well and know how to keep the sort of open mind that allows new insights to form. The more threatened or impatient we are, the more we rush to judgment. In practice, that means that we confirm our own opinions. The consequence is that we inhibit our ability to form new insights. That is why neuropsychologist Karl Pribram advocates what he calls "active uncertainty." It means deliberately suspending judgment while actively investigating the subject or issue in question.

Here are some questions to serve as indicators for you and others:

How quickly do you form impressions about people? About new ideas?

How important is it for you to have immediate answers to questions?

How much time do you willingly take to work on something that you do not understand?

How easy is it for you to "let an idea go"?

Commentary

There is a difference between having an open mind and thinking that we have an open mind. Each of us is— or has—a self. That means that we have acquired an extensive set of values and beliefs that define what we regard as real and important. Students also have such a set of beliefs. The tendency is to deny or reject what conflicts with our inner reality or to interpret what is new so as to reduce it to what we already know.

It is extremely important that we create an atmosphere in which "not knowing" and "being confused" can be positive experiences. They are the gates through which we pass from what was known to what is learned.

Implications for Education

There is an interplay between conscious and unconscious. Our job is to help our students use their conscious minds in order to facilitate and access unconscious processing. This approach to teaching involves both attitudes and skills. However, the rewards are enormous because such an approach bypasses the bottlenecks of short-term memory and attention and engages the enormous reserve capacities in every mind.

This attitude is as important as it is difficult to develop. It takes confidence in ourselves and our work. We must believe that answers will be found and that sense will emerge eventually. In other words, we need to have confidence in unconscious processing.

We have to realize that students will be depending on and activating their current sets of values and pre-dispositions, together with their dreams, drives, and purposes. We call these values and dreams "deep meanings." They are what each of us lives for. Meaningful learning inevitably engages and expands deep meanings. This is the way to fulfillment in learning and teaching.

Educators must be aware both of the process and of their own deep meanings. We cannot help others to grow if we cannot or will not be aware of deep meanings, which is why we begin this book with an in-depth exploration of

Notes

what it means to learn. Among other things, good teachers are people who know themselves. They also realize that because meaningful learning changes the self, what students are really acquiring through their education is self-knowledge.

Here are some questions to guide you.

1. **Do your students suddenly show that they learned something when you were beginning to doubt that it had sunk in?**

2. **Do student understandings ever show up in unexpected contexts?**

3. **Have you ever seen students mull over or persist with a project long after they might be expected to move onto something else?**

4. **Do you ever ask questions or generate projects that lead to ongoing student interest over a long period of time?**

5. **Do your students ever bring unsolicited new material or information to you in response to a project or subject that you have all been exploring together?**

Stable systems resist change;
dynamic systems exist by changing

14

Priniciple Nine

We Have at Least Two Types of Memory— A Spatial Memory System and a Set of Systems for Rote Learning

Memory is a very complex function, and it engages all of our abilities and mental, emotional, and physical systems. O'Keefe and Nadel (1978) have demonstrated that the brain organizes memory in at least two different ways. Although the systems interact, their different qualities are extremely important.

One set of systems is specifically designed for the organization, storage, and retrieval of relatively unrelated information. The generic name for all these systems is *taxon memory*. ("Taxon" was coined in the 1970s; it is based on "taxonomy.")

Another system monitors our moment-to-moment move through space and time and is designed for registering our ordinary experiences. It is called the "locale system" (from "location.") We touched on this system with the reference to autobiographical memory in Principle One, and we expand upon it here.

As you will see, it is partly the characteristics of these two systems that explain why teaching for meaning is so very different from teaching for memorization.

Spatial or Autobiographical Memory

We have in common with other animals at least one memory system, the locale memory system, which is designed to help us navigate in space and time.

Activity

Think of an animal that is ready to walk around within hours of its birth. A horse, for example, once it can stand, begins to move about in the barn or open field where it was born. No one instructed it about depth perception, moving in space, and avoiding walls and fences.

Question: Which other animals have similar abilities?

Answer: Several, including human beings!

In some animals this memory system is fully formed at birth, but such is not the case with humans. However, we are also genetically endowed with the natural capacity to navigate in space and time. You needed to be in a new place for only a short time in order to be able to recall many features without using memorization or repeated rehearsal.

Activity

Step 1   Recall the last time you visited a new theater or went into a friend's home for the first time. How easy was it to get a sense of the layout so that, for instance, you could find the restroom and then find your way back? Could you still find your way around that place? Did you have to rehearse or memorize to do this?

Step 2   In your mind's eye, trace the path from your home to the nearest shopping center. Be aware of how much detail is actually stored in your memory.

Autobiographical Memories as Maps

The system is important because our locale memories operate as dynamic or changing maps. Think about it. We use that ongoing, detailed sensory picture to help us find our way or to learn our way no matter where we are. Moreover, we also have to know where we are in time. For instance, we might ask whether it is time to have breakfast or to read this book or to prepare for class. Those are questions that we use to find our way in time.

That ongoing space-time map is experienced by us as our life story; the system is actually accumulating autobiographical memories. It is this mapping function that is so vital. It may be very rich, or it may be rather impoverished, depending upon such factors as our capacity to perceive sensory detail. That is why we have included in this book some exercises for enhancing sensory awareness.

Activity

Take some time to recollect the major events in the last six months of your life.

Where were you? What did you do?

Note the way in which you think chronologically in order to recall items that have faded.

Also, what memories were "automatic" in that they did not require memorization or rehearsal?

Notes

Characteristics of the Locale Memory System

There are several important characteristics of this system. You can test them by self-observation.

1. **It is almost inexhaustible.**
   It operates from morning to night for a lifetime. (Except, perhaps, when you might have been totally exhausted, has there ever been a time when you have been in a new place and made NO attempt to orient yourself?)

2. **Because it must adjust to new situations immediately it is innately motivated by novelty.**
   (Do you ever spontaneously pay attention to significant events or new people that move into your life space?)

3. **The locale system calls upon all the mind-body systems.**
   The quality and duration of the maps are very much influenced by sensory awareness and emotional intensity. The more "present" we are in some context, the more complete is the map. (Is there an emotional event in your past that you still remember very vividly?)

4. **We form short-term maps instantly, as well as others that last for a very long time.**
   It is the locale memory system that explains why authentic experience is so important in education. When we orchestrate the immersion of learners in multiple, complex, real-life experiences, we naturally engage their own life stories and life context. This is crucial in helping them to make sense of what it is that we seek to teach.

The Taxon Systems

Not all new information comes to us naturally. Relatively meaningless information is usually retained through effort and by rote. This rote-learned information includes procedures and behaviors such as teaching a child to wash his or her hands after going to the bathroom or looking both ways before crossing the street.

Memories that are stored in these systems tend to be automatic and repeatable even under pressure. They do not need to make sense or be reasonable. In fact, one of the interesting things about taxon systems is that they can be programmed very much like a computer to produce the same response over and over, unconnected to other information or to the context or ongoing events. That also has some drawbacks, as we will see.

Some of the early work on memory involved the recall of nonsense syllables. A list might look like this:

qwa	mir
pol	yoz
brk	erp

Activity

How would you remember these syllables?

If you had a list of twenty, how long would it take to remember them?

What would motivate you to remember them?

How long do you think your memory of them would last?

One reason the syllables can be remembered is that the taxon memory systems are specifically designed for recording information that does not make any sense or is not natural or meaningful.

Characteristics of the Taxon Memory Systems

The qualities of taxon systems should not be surprising.

1. They do fatigue, and therefore rest is needed between intervals of memorization and rehearsal.

2. They are susceptible to extrinsic motivation. This means that rewards and punishments wielded by others can induce memorization.

Are these qualities consistent with your experiences with rote learning?

Importance of the Taxon Systems

1. Taxon systems can ultimately serve to enrich our natural spatial memory. Thus, we can hold meaningless, memorized information in storage until it makes sense. One example might be procedures that we learn for operating a computer.

2. The systems can be counted on not to change during times of fear or pressure. Think of a fireman in danger, a soldier who must remember very specific firing procedures, or a musician who must perform a specific piece of music at a concert.

Activity

In your experience, what sorts of taxon memories might be very important to the survival of a human adult or child? (Example: look before you cross the street.)

What initially meaningless memories have you stored that have ultimately become meaningful?

Taxon Maps

Taxon maps are very different from locale maps. They are static and are built via many memorized routes. It's a little like building a house from a kit by memorizing or by having detailed instructions for each of the steps or procedures.

Such memory requires that we have a map or plan of the job to begin with (there is a predetermined outcome). We also have specific procedures to follow, some of which may have to be practiced and rehearsed along the way.

What are the advantages of building a house this way?

What might be the disadvantages?

What would be the primary way of teaching workers to build such a house?

How would they be motivated?

Commentary

A great deal of education results in the acquisition by students of complex maps of this kind. Even critical thinking skills can be learned in this way. The problem is that these maps are extremely inflexible. For example, a student may learn complex math procedures and yet be incapable of using them in real life, say at a checkout counter or in talking to a banker about finances. Thus, rote learning is extremely ineffective for the development of natural knowledge and is one of the primary reasons so many of our students cannot think.

Implications for Teaching

Both memory systems are important. In fact they interact all the time in the natural operation of the brain. It is important that we grasp their different properties very clearly, because the conditions that we set up for learners will determine how the two systems are used.

If, for example, we build a context that is driven by externally controlled rewards and punishments, students will engage in two types of learning. They will use their taxon systems for the rote memory of the information about which they feel threatened (usually course content). Its meaningfulness will be irrelevant. They will also be constructing life maps geared toward their survival. In other words, they will be learning about their environment. This may show up in their ability to "read" the teacher, manipulate their peers, and so on.

We do not want robots who execute rote memories of course content. Ultimately we want people to have complex, flexible maps of learning that allow them to change course if the context requires it. To do that, students must learn for meaningfulness, and that requires the use of their locale memory system in conjunction with the new information.

Here are some guidelines, in the form of questions, that will help you to establish the conditions in which locale mapping is encouraged.

1. **Do you plan for and allow students many opportunities to do tasks for which they are intrinsically motivated?**

2. **Are students given choices for activities whenever possible?**

3. **Do you make every effort to help them link to and build on what they already know?**

4. **Are you rarely happy teaching material that has no meaning for students?**

5. **How do time constraints tend to favor the programming of taxon memories?**

Everything is connected

15

Principle Ten

The Brain Understands and Remembers Best When Facts and Skills Are Embedded in Natural Spatial Memory

Although we have more than one kind of memory system, the systems are deeply interconnected, and that interconnectedness must be employed in teaching for meaning. We have to acknowledge and capitalize on a student's autobiographical memory. When we talk of natural autobiographical memory, we talk of engaging every body-mind system naturally.

When educators embed new facts and skills in a living context, students learn prescribed content in the way that they acquire all other natural knowledge, such as their native language. In effect, educators support the marriage between content and context.

Some time ago the navy was training mechanics to repair carburetors. The instructors taught the appropriate procedures and skills by having mechanics operate on one carburetor in a particular vehicle. Mechanics ended up fixing this particular carburetor at high levels of proficiency. Problems occurred, however, when the mechanics were asked to work on other types of carburetors in other vehicles. They had memorized specific procedures and skills—routes—for one specific outcome. They had not acquired a general understanding of how a carburetor works.

What the Navy had to do was to start virtually from scratch and teach the mechanics how carburetors fit into the entire scheme of an engine—what their function is, how carburetors relate to other parts—not as static entities, but as parts of a system (map) that can change (from vehicle to vehicle).

There are many degrees of sophistication in embedding new content in autobiographical memory. We would like to move through several stages here by way of illustration. We will begin with a complex philosophical issue because the principle applies to everything from vocational skills to philosophy.

Activity

Here is an introduction to the philosopher Plato.

1. **Plato's main idea**

   Plato believed that the material universe is imperfect. All material objects and all our systems and values are images and approximations of universal ideal forms, such as "justice" or "the perfect triangle." People are essentially confused and blinded by illusions instead of being aware of what is real. Although our capacity to grasp these forms is limited, the role of education is to help people steadily move closer to the reality of these ideals.

   Note your thoughts—including whether you currently agree or disagree with Plato or whether you even have a feeling for what he might mean. Note also your interest, your likelihood of remembering, and other observations that seem important to you.

2. Plato's use of parables to illustrate his ideas

The "Allegory of the Cave" was intended to make it easier to understand his idea.

Imagine a group of people confined to the darkness of a cave for their entire lives. They are bound in such a way that they cannot move their heads from one side to the other, nor can they walk about. Suppose that in this condition their guards build a fire regularly and objects that pass in front of the fire cast shadows on the wall in front of the prisoners. The shadows on the wall are the only reality the prisoners know. Plato asks us to imagine that the prisoners spend the time identifying the shadows, predicting things about them, and inventing clever games. It is all they know of reality. Moreover, if someone were to get free of the cave, grasp the truth, and return to share that truth with the prisoners, that person would probably be ridiculed.

Discuss and note your reactions to the use of the allegory. Does it make Plato's idea more vivid? More understandable?

Commentary

The use of a story or parable creates immediate images for us. We can reconstruct a story more easily than we can remember abstract content or information. Stories and parables have been associated with the world's greatest teachers. The story allows many truths to be expressed.

3. **Finding other ways to explore Plato's ideas**

   Consider and discuss reenacting Plato's allegory, perhaps literally, perhaps through some artistic expression. What would you do? What would be the point of emphasis?

Role-play being Plato and some of his students

Wear some clothing that gives an indication of the time.

Test Plato's ideas

Imagine being in ancient Greece and debating which is more "real"—the number 7 or a table in the room. Try to build as many arguments as you can to support each position.

Commentary

By creating our own expression of the story, we immediately engage in interpretive thinking. We also begin to relate to the ideas more personally. The more activities of this kind that we employ, the more the whole atmosphere now becomes more lifelike. People take on personalities, use language, participate in community affairs, wear clothing, and use their imaginations and their senses. The intellectual discussion, which is extremely important, is embedded in these complex social activities. The use of analogies, stories, and special activities also helps to create a more real and vivid context. Not only will particular facts be learned more easily and be retained longer, but also the activity allows individuals to build their own meanings into the experience and the content.

Activity

Begin to explore other ways in which new information is embedded in real or imaginary complex experience. Here are some examples:

- Shelly Duvall's "It's a Bird's Life" is a software program for young children that takes them on a wacky trip into the Amazon. The program includes bird noises and other sounds. An x-ray machine lets children see the bones of birds. There are some sixty screens through which the children can click onto various activities.

- A teacher wants to cover the operation of the human heart. She uses a combination of the movie *Inner Space* and Isaac Asimov's *Incredible Journey* to set up an imaginary journey by a team of investigators through someone's heart. Blood pressure, the position and path of arteries and veins, and other aspects of the heart's operation have to be dealt with by specific members of the team, such as the navigator or the pilot.

- A corporate training company has developed an accounting game to teach basic accounting to people in business, which it does by inviting all the adults to pretend to be ten years old again and to set up a lemonade stand.

- A tenth-grade science teacher decides to introduce his chemistry course by dressing up as a dentist for the animals for the local zoo. One of his first clients is the elephant, for whom he has to manufacture a special toothpaste.

Following are some questions for discussion:

What do these scenarios have in common?

How much information could be embedded in these scenarios?

How much could the classroom be decorated to make the experiences come alive?

How could you use stories and projects initiated or designed by students themselves to embed the content that you wish to teach?

In your group, discuss or invent possible scenarios that you could use.

Implications for Teaching

Natural mapping involves all the body-mind systems operating in "natural" ways. This process is rich and complex. It is not a matter of using a few techniques for generating interest. Rather, it is a matter of "getting into" an appropriate life space.

Again, envision the process of natural mapping in terms of how we learn our native language: the dress, the rituals, the people, the ongoing events, the ceremonies, the music, the multiplicity of parallel events, and much more. Mapping depends on the richness as well as the coherence of the experience.

We have traditionally deprived students because we have regarded as irrelevant most of the information that is essential for a sense of meaningfulness. We have broken content into fragments that become more difficult to deal with simply because of the inappropriate fragmentation.

Notes

The key is to work at two levels. First, it is necessary to be imaginative with the content of the course. Second, a natural and living atmosphere is vital. We refer to this as orchestrating the immersion of the learner in multiple, complex, interactive experiences.

Following are guidelines in the form of questions to assist you.

1. **Do I use stories and illustrations in my teaching that create mental pictures?**

2. **Do I use concrete objects as illustrations or metaphors for abstract concepts?**

3. **Do I create experiences for students that embed the content in activity or artistic expression?**

4. **Do I establish a classroom setting that reflects what is being studied and is consistent with the way it is being studied?**

5. **Do I encourage students to create their own modes of expression (for example, their own questions, their own tests, their own projects, their own applications)?**

6. **Do I plan lessons that involve reenactment of particular concepts?**

7. **Do I go outside of the classroom into the real world?**

8. **Do I create real world dilemmas that relate what is being learned to the human experience?**

9. **Do I use language in many different ways?**

Rhythms and cycles are present everywhere

16

Principle Eleven

Learning Is Enhanced by Challenge and Inhibited by Threat

Watching someone become red with embarrassment or feeling our hands become icy before a public talk is so common to us that we do not see it as a significant event. But what we are observing are actually indicators of subtle changes occurring in the rest of the physiology, including the brain, as the result of perceived threat. The brain appears to be very much like a camera lens which opens to receive information when challenged, interested or when in an "innocent", child-like mode, and closes when we perceive threat that triggers fear.

— Caine and Caine, *Making Connections*

In our terms, a threat is anything that triggers a sense of helplessness. It is accompanied by the perceptual narrowing called "downshifting." The body then reverts to very primitive survival instincts and procedures. These include rote learned procedures and beliefs—surface knowledge—that are stored in the taxon systems. In addition, the locale memory system becomes less effective, and people actually lose contact with some of their own memories and capabilities. It then becomes extremely difficult to use the autobiographical memory system effectively. The acquisition of natural knowledge is then significantly impeded. These changes also occur as a result of extreme fatigue.

Challenge has a very different effect from that of threat. It involves a combination of personal interest or intrinsic motivation together with a sense of empowerment—the feeling that "I can do it." It is in these circumstances that complex and creative patterning becomes possible.

Threat is induced, a feeling of helplessness is created, and people are demotivated when others specify a closed set of permissible outcomes and then seek to enforce them through a combination of rewards and punishments. (For the research on this phenomenon, see *Making Connections*, chapters 6 and 10.) These conditions describe much of what happens in education. This approach is based on some assumptions about how people function and learn that must be changed.

Activity

Can you remember when you were a new teacher or administrator walking into a classroom for the first time? How did you feel?

Have you ever, as a result of some transgression, been hauled before some authority who had real power to affect your results or your future? How did you feel?

Have you ever been free to experiment with your teaching in a subject that you loved and with students that you believed in? What happened?

Have you ever experienced having no one believe in you and then having someone genuinely believe in and support you? Did it make a difference?

Commentary

Downshifting is real. It means reverting to primitive programs and following old beliefs and behaviors regardless of what information the "road signs" in the actual context provide. Responses become more automatic and limited. It is a matter of not being able to access all that one knows or to see what is really there. It is accompanied by a reduction in one's ability to take into consideration subtle—and sometimes obvious—environmental and internal cues and make genuine creative links.

A story is told about some pioneers driving covered wagons into areas of southern Africa where they had never before been. At a rest place, one person went off to hunt. Some hours later his friends were surprised to see him cross their path, and then do so again, without acknowledging them. Then it dawned on one of them. The hunter was lost! He was so deeply absorbed in his fear of being lost and his desire to return that he did not realize he was traveling in circles, nor did he see his friends when they were nearby.

Downshifting appears to result in a reduced capacity to engage in complex intellectual functioning illustrated by a loss of creativity and the ability to engage in open-ended thinking and questioning. Indeed, much behavior and thinking can become phobic in the sense that specific stimuli trigger instant, potentially inappropriate, and usually exaggerated responses.

One result is clear. If we want to facilitate learning that makes maximum connections for the learner, such learning requires the learner to be actively and intrinsically motivated. Punishments, quick rewards, or conditions that take the initiative away from learners and make them helpless pawns will force them into routine solutions. Students will abort trying to make complex connections, and they will revert to narrow survival programs.

Activity

Think of a project that you want to complete. It can be something you need to learn, but it should be one that requires you to make connections with what you already know.

Write the title of the project here:

_____

Now visualize working on your project under two different sets of conditions, as follows:

1. **Your project must be completed according to a set of severe constraints. For instance,**

   - You have a time line that scares you.

   - Not doing this project will result in some form of real loss to you.

   - Doing the project could bring major rewards (money, promotion, recognition, and so on)

   - The project is not your own idea; someone else assigned it to you.

   - The outcome has been pre-specified by someone. The objectives have been determined for you. You know that there is a "right" way and a "wrong" way to do it.

What would your state of mind be? How would you feel about doing this project? How enthusiastic would you be? How creative would you be? How much of a risk would you take?

2. **You have a significant degree of control and choice in designing and completing the project. For instance,**

- This is your project; you initiated it and wanted to be involved.

- There may be rewards down the road, but basically you are doing it for the sheer fun of it.

- You can go down some experimental roads in your search for answers and you have the time to explore.

- You have the time and the resources available to do a thorough job.

What would doing the project be like under these conditions? How would you feel about doing this project? How enthusiastic would you be? How creative would you be? How much of a risk would you take?

Commentary

Notice that you may experience some stress in both conditions but that they are qualitatively different. Any time we are placed under stress that involves some degree of helplessness (generally meaning that someone else is in charge), we tend to do only what needs to be done. What is also critical is that under these conditions we tend to be much less motivated for future, related types of activities or learning. What we experience is what Hans Selye, the father of stress research, called distress. This debilitating form of stress weakens our physiology, particularly our immune system. Over time, this type of stress reaction also affects our moods, patience, ability to demonstrate affection, and other behaviors.

If, on the other hand, we experience intrinsic motivation and we are in charge of finding solutions, then we are also under stress, but it is what Selye called *eustress* (from "euphoria"). That kind of stress is far less debilitating, and we recover quickly from any negative physiological damage. Some research also suggests that these types of projects leave us ready to do more work (see *Growing Up Creative* by Teresa Amabile, 1989).

Notice that if you wanted to be particularly creative or come up with unique solutions, you absolutely needed the second set of circumstances. Creativity research suggests that truly creative projects are difficult, if not impossible, to do under the first set of conditions outlined above (see *Making Connections*).

The issue becomes more complex, however, if we see that some restrictive elements can be well tolerated if we are working on a final goal or long-term outcome we have chosen for ourselves.

Notes

Implications for Teaching

Most people know that distress has a debilitating effect on health. What has not been recognized is that it also inhibits learning and the functioning of intelligence.

The conditions in which we find it difficult to think quickly or be creative also apply to our students. Because threat reduces creativity, and because meaningful learning is inherently creative, we must generate an atmosphere that is low in threat and high in challenge.

Here are some indicators of a threatening context for us:

1. The boss or teacher wants it completed, irrespective of what we desire.

2. There are stringent time limits.

3. The project is closely linked to rewards or punishment (such as money or a grade) controlled by others.

4. The outcome is totally pre-specified.

These conditions are compatible with learning that focuses on memorization or rehearsal. They also work in many instances for engaging preprogrammed skills and knowledge. Rote types of skills can be learned or called on when creative projects and solutions, open-ended thinking, discovery, and higher order thinking such as analysis, synthesis, and critical thinking, are inhibited

Here are some indicators of a challenging context:

1. There is a significant degree of personal interest in the selection of a project.

2. Much of the reward lies in the creativity and experience of the project itself.

3. A significant portion of the project is open-ended, both in terms of time constraints and possible outcomes.

The optimal state of mind for learning, that of relaxed alertness, flourishes in a low-threat, high-challenge environment, particularly when supplemented by the wellness we talk about in Principle Two. We will deal with this optimal state in depth in a future book on the subject. In the meantime there are some excellent exercises in appendix C to help you on your way.

The whole is contained in every part

17

Principle Twelve
Each Brain Is Unique

Every brain is uniquely organized so there are no two people exactly alike. However, there are similar patterns or configurations in perception. For example, in Principle Eleven we point out that all people learn best in a low-threat, high-challenge environment. However, what constitutes threat or challenge varies. Some people actually like mountain climbing and hang gliding, whereas others are distinctly ill at ease in such environments.

There are many approaches to the art of assessing individual differences. One way is to build profiles of people through observation and by using a specific set of questions.

Activity
Assessing Differences

You may ask selected people these questions directly, answer the questions on the basis of your knowledge about them, or do both and compare the results.

- Are you strongly influenced by what is going on around you, or do you maintain your own goals and manner?

Notes

- Are you responsive to people and emotions, or do you tend to be factual, analytical, or detached?

- Is it more important for you to think about a task or to do it?

- Do you have a good sense of location in physical space?

- Do you incorporate music into your life? What sort? When?

- Do you have insight into your own values and patterns?

- What sorts of food do you like?

- When are you interested? Entertained? Bored?

Commentary

It is because there are so many variables that we can say that everyone is alike and that everyone is different. There are also many cultural characteristics, which you might like to explore for yourself, that both unite people and separate them. Our challenge is to understand and appreciate those similarities and differences.

One way of helping people to grasp differences is to identify different learning or personality styles. There are many instruments on the market for doing this. We have developed our own, which we find extremely useful in helping people to appreciate their own ways of perceiving reality and processing information and input. We have outlined four different types of perceptual preference in appendix B of this workbook.

Activity

Making Differences Meaningful

It is important to appreciate people's unique approaches to creating meaning. Some excellent lessons are provided by trying to walk a mile in someone else's moccasins. Here are some processes to explore:

1. We have suggested that you keep a journal of your thoughts and reflections as you examine this book. If you trust one another enough, exchange books and journals. What do you notice about your colleague?

2. Live someone else's life for a while—even in small ways. Reduce your discretionary spending by 50 percent for one week (if you can). Exchange housekeeping roles with your husband or wife for a week. Select a philosopher or psychologist who has a prescription for living—and practice some aspect of that prescription diligently. Take a weekend course, but adopt a new name and background, and don't let anyone know. Record what happens.

Notes

Implications for Teaching

If meaningful learning is inherently creative, then we must create the conditions under which people can find their own solutions. We need to be able to help them do it and appreciate their creativity, which can be difficult at the best of times. It is even more difficult when we are under pressure to produce results.

However, once we do get a handle on the richly diverse array of talents and beliefs that are present in any classroom, we have a chance to see the differences as resources and not obstacles. In effect, using individuality well becomes a way of generating much better results.

There is an additional benefit. Our ability to recognize and liberate diversity will be reflected in our capacity to call upon a wider array of our own skills and abilities. We grow as we help our students grow. We become creative in helping them to be creative. We recognize their uniqueness and we find our individuality.

Here are some questions to guide your exploration of this principle:

1. How is diversity defined from the point of view of the brain?

2. How does complex teaching help individuals express their unique talents?

3. What is individuality? Is it real?

4. What does it mean to understand and develop our unique selves?

5. In what ways are we unique individuals while being the same as others?

6. How are we all connected?

PART III

Making It Happen

The brain does the learning. Our job is to help it. It can record nonsense. It can also make sense. The conditions that we set up govern which of the two prevails. One outcome is the expansion of natural knowledge and a great deal of personal growth as well. The other outcome is surface knowledge and a largely impoverished spirit.

The practical consequence of education is that we are creating and shaping human beings. The only purpose that we regard as acceptable is to enhance and expand the human beings in our care as much as possible.

The question, now, is how to get beyond surface knowledge to the expansion of natural knowledge. We begin with a reexamination of the nature of meaning.

18

Teaching for Meaning

Assume, for a moment, that you are training a chef. What does this person need to know and be able to do?

A friend of yours, Michale, is a gourmet chef who comes to mind as a model because he has a superb "sense" or "feel" for cooking. Rather than just measuring ingredients precisely, he sometimes modifies quantities because it seems right. In addition to using the basic ingredients, he can add spices and flavorings and adjust them to suit the guests. Michale can move about the kitchen easily and seems to juggle several steps at one time. And when there is a problem, he is skilled at recovering. Michale has what you know to be a "felt meaning."

Obviously, your trainee needs to have access to recipes, know how to buy or obtain essential ingredients, and have the skill to use appropriate equipment such as ovens. All of this is equivalent to the basic information and procedures of any subject that a student learns.

In addition, there is something more. In almost every case, the potential chef must, like Michale, want to be a gourmet cook. There is a goal or drive or urge in that person. It helps him or her to be commited and to understand. The goal may include a dream about the way that he or she will be able to entertain. It keeps the person going during the tough times and contributes to the sheer joy gained from good results and the interest the chef may have in meals that "fail." This inner drive is part of the potential chef's "deep meaning."

Felt Meaning: The "Aha!" of Insight

We all know what it is like to have a flash of insight or understanding—when things come together and make sense. Look at the picture. What do you see? (Our answer is at the end of the chapter.)

This exercise is basically one in visual perception, but the same thing happens with all our other senses. There is a coming together of parts in a way that "fits." We might experience felt meaning when a poem that we are reading begins to make sense. We might also feel this way

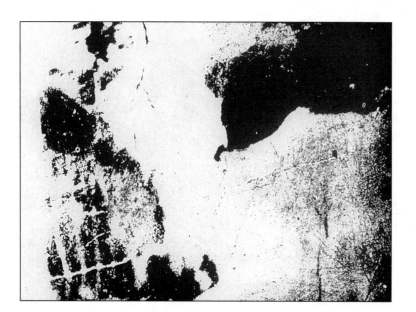

when a learning experience that we have orchestrated falls into place or we find a way to solve a complex administrative problem.

A frequently remarked-on experience is the sense of relief and energy that often accompanies this type of insight. Sometimes the sensation is very slight. Other insights evoke emotions ranging from awe to an almost mystical sense of oneness to joy and delight.

Recall some insights that you have had and how you felt.

Real insights change the way that we look at the world. They change our perception. That is what happens when, say, computing begins to make sense, or we finally "see" what an author was trying to say.

When we have these experiences, we are actually changing inside. Usually we have expanded a previous way of perceiving something, which is very different from memorizing. When we memorize something, we can store it without understanding it. We can also recall it when the right question is asked. When we develop felt meaning, however, we relate more effectively to procedures and information.

Recall some of these major changes in yourself. For example, compare the first time you entered a classroom with the way you do it now. How much more is familiar now? How do you know what to expect of a particular day or class?

Recall the first time you studied a subject that you now know very well. What are the differences in the way that you deal with the subject matter? Note that taking things for granted is often an indicator that one has a felt meaning for it. It shows that you either have or are acquiring natural knowledge.

Think about an ongoing relationship that you have. Do you now recognize the signs that your partner is upset? Happy? Are there moments when you can predict what he or she will do without being told? What else has changed?

You may have noticed that learning like this takes time. It does not happen readily under the pressure of time.

Commentary

Felt meaning is the first key to developing new natural knowledge. Felt meaning engages all the brain/mind systems. One reason for using the word *felt* is that there is much more than merely linguistic or "cognitive" functioning. The "felt" part becomes our intuitive link between information, our values, and previous knowledge.

In the face of objectives, textual content, and testing requirements, we often forget that it is this spark of insight we see in students' faces that keeps us going. Without that, we may find teaching a hopeless endeavor.

As an exercise, you might like to refer back to the brain principles and explore the number of operations that are involved in meaningful learning. There are sensory, emotional, and physiological components to meaning. You will find attention and peripheral perception, multiple levels of sensory input, focused attention and unconscious processing, the interrelations of parts and wholes, a much greater capacity to have insights when not feeling threatened or helpless, unique ways of approaching the same problem, a significant flow and range of emotional involvement, and more.

Meaningful learning really is a whole body-mind process. Felt meaning is experienced as the coming together of those operations. It is absolutely indispensable for the generation of natural knowledge. Thus, meaningful learning *must* be seen as a creative process. Students must have permission to go beyond the specific objectives of their teachers. They also must have the open psychological space that is essential for creativity.

Deep Meanings: The Driving Force

Of course, there is more to learning than surface knowledge and felt meaning. There is also what drives us. We call these forces *deep meanings*. Deep meanings are at the heart of intrinsic motivation, because they are the sum of what is important to us. Deep meanings include what we already know or have learned—those things to which we are committed and that have become part of us, including, therefore, our current natural knowledge.

Attempts to Systematize Motivation

We are simply pointing out that every human mind harbors complex values and beliefs that govern what is perceived to be important. Abraham Maslow suggested that every human being has a hierarchy of motives and that needs that are lower on the list must be satisfied before the higher ones become operative. From higher to lower, Maslow lists these needs:

Self-actualization and personal growth

Ego needs

Social needs, including belonging

Safety needs

Physical survival needs

Maslow's theory is much more complex than we are presenting here, but this brief sketch nevertheless offers a useful way of appreciating the range of inner drives we all have.

The Power of Individual Purpose

George Kelly believed that everyone is different and that we all combine ideas in our own way. Hence he developed the theory that we could identify the individual "constructs" of each person, and the constructs would reveal what is and is not important to that person.

In teaching for meaning it is important to realize that meaning develops within an individual as he or she interacts with knowledge and experience. Meaning is enveloped in ideas that live on in our lives. In fact, ideas live for generations. They become values and concepts that shape our everyday existence.

Ideas can become more important to us than life itself. Think of the concepts *freedom, love,* and *right and wrong.* These can provide for us the very purpose for living. One of the great joys of teaching is in sharing what is meaningful to us in ways that help students glimpse the excitement, usefulness, and relevance of knowledge to their own lives.

Education is all about making ideas meaningful in our lives. Somehow, because ideas are not measurable in classical ways, we have substituted information and surface knowledge rather than meaning as the essence of teaching. We have reasoned that if we know enough "stuff," ideas and meaning will follow. However, that just hasn't happened and isn't likely to.

Deep meanings bring purpose to experience. They are extremely powerful in hindering or driving a person. In fact, deep meanings actually guide the selection of many of the experiences that we have, the way those experiences are perceived, and the value we place on them. We must pay attention to the deep meanings of our students.

Compile a list of the ideas that guide you, such as your political philosophy or religious convictions, and the persistent desires and fears that you have. (Examples: "I want to live in the mountains" or "I am fearful of old age.")

How do these influence what you study, read, look for, prefer?

In what way do they enrich your life?

Commentary

Deep meanings are the second key to developing new natural knowledge. Much of what is represented by deep meanings is apparent in the brain principles. For example, we suggest in *Making Connections* that there are two survival principles. The first is flight or fight, which is represented at the base of Maslow's hierarchy. The second is self-reorganization through learning, which is reflected in Maslow's notion of self-actualization. The locale memory system, which generates our life maps, is intrinsically motivated by novelty—and what each person finds novel is unique.

We have also explored the importance of emotion in each human, and emotions are expressed in egoic, social, and creative spheres. They provide direction and energy for what actually becomes natural knowledge. They are always operative. At a minimum they must be acknowledged. In practice, they must be accessed. Deep meanings have a fundamental role in the shape and structure of the self, because they also set up the barriers to what a person can or cannot, will or will not learn.

Natural Knowledge Revisited

If all that students do is remember and store information, then all that they acquire is surface knowledge. They need more. Students need to acquire the frames of reference, the tools for understanding, and the creative ability to be successful in the information age. Moreover, these must be second nature if they are to be used readily in a variety of contexts. The goal for education must be the expansion of natural knowledge.

Acquiring natural knowledge is very different from memorization. We need to integrate surface knowledge, felt meaning, and deep meaning. The process is somewhat like a chemical reaction, with natural knowledge as the product. It is the way knowledge interacts with our experience that allows us to build meaningful ideas and values.

information + felt meaning + deep meaning = expansion of natural knowledge

Have you ever wondered why first- and second-graders almost universally love to study dinosaurs? Children learn incredibly difficult names, the habitats, and identifying characteristics. It seems that the more they learn, the more they want to know. Is it the knowledge about dinosaurs itself that creates this excitement, or could it be the "idea" of the dinosaur?

The idea of huge creatures stimulates an imaginary world inside the child that just keeps going. Students draw pictures, play make-believe with small model dinosaurs, hug stuffed replicas, and re-create an imaginary existence of their own making. By mediating the factual world of dinosaur information and the imaginative world of the child, one can observe the relationship of knowledge and meaning.

You can add more and more "facts" as long as you keep the "idea" of dinosaurs alive for children. Once the idea is squelched, however, the facts lose their fascination. Meaning is lost.

To keep meaning alive, we must remember some important principles:

1. All learning is developmental, as we point out in part 1 of this workbook. This fact is true for our students as well as for us. The developmental nature of learning means that natural knowledge is being formed all the time. Acquiring natural knowledge does not just happen on schedule in a classroom. Genuine learning takes time.

2. Natural knowledge is formed when many different aspects of experience are tied together. It never forms easily when we keep each subject separate from others and separate from life.

3. Natural knowledge forms uniquely inside each learner. The ways in which patterns come together vary, even if people find the same solutions to problems.

4. Every student must be permitted to come to this mastery in his or her own way. Meanings are unique, even if outcomes are similar.

5. We must always teach for more than our intended outcomes. When the possibilities are rich, students have the opportunity to explore content creatively. Such exploration is what they have to do to acquire natural knowledge.

Review: How to Teach for the Expansion of Natural Knowledge

Once we know what our learner looks like, and that, according to the principles, our learner is actively engaged in making meaning of what he or she is experiencing, then we are ready to look at teaching.

Notes

Notes

When we teach for the expansion of natural knowledge we take students beyond their present understanding and beliefs, and we cannot use mere memorization of information or acquisition of meaningless skills to take them there. Students must have the opportunity to question, to practice, to demonstrate, to apply, to critique, to describe opposites and take on board new concepts, and to teach what they have learned to others.

Children who study democracy in order to pass a test or a course are different from those who understand democracy in action and know how they fit into a democratic society because they have experienced government in action. The latter have been participants in a democratic process or institution.

Recent curriculum developments in science, mathematics, and the social sciences emphasize active learning in a way that combines content, thinking skills, and creativity. Although active learning is nothing new, the intellectual requirements of students have been expanded to include both disciplinary and real-world applications. Authentic assessments place a new kind of pressure on teachers somehow to bring all this together in a way that satisfies every constituency.

Teachers frequently acknowledge that students are much more engaged when involved in activities. Active learning generally increases students' motivation and excitement for learning. Such motivation and excitement indicates that relaxed alertness is being achieved. But is that enough? A question that plagues many teachers is "Are they learning what they are 'supposed' to be learning?" This question is complex when our perspective includes the whole brain.

The fact is, experiential learning increases the complexity of the instructional process. Paradoxically, though, as purposeful complexity increases, so does the potential for learning. For example, when students are engaged in an open-ended, creative exploration of a problem or topic, they will very often go in many different directions. Or they will perceive a rather wide set of understandings that may seem to be exceedingly disparate and unconnected. How does a teacher help students to consolidate, organize, and make sense out of the collections of meanings that have been constructed? How can the teacher relate this wide range of meanings to curriculum expectations?

These questions surely relate to a new understanding of our roles as teachers and to new skills that help us be effective in a complex, open environment. In brain-based instruction, the teacher perceives her or his role as one who orchestrates experience and who draws from the collection of meanings that are created by the students. This means that the teacher never controls everything that happens in the classroom; rather, it implies that he or she sets into motion a wide range of connected experiences or occasions for learning and actively observes, directs, and engages the learning processes.

Specifically, we call this *active processing*. As you work through this book, you will begin to employ many different ways of thinking about your own classroom. You will reflect on your own insights and meanings as well as those of others in your group. Active processing is a means of organizing and exploring ever more deeply the meanings and understandings we generate. Begin to notice all the ways that you try to understand experience. Remember, complex experience is natural; it is isolating and fragmenting experience that is arbitrary and artificial. Understanding and building upon how the brain operates naturally can help us understand what our role in the classroom must be and leads to the expansion of natural knowledge.

Summary

There is a way to teach for meaning and for the expansion of natural knowledge. The features of that way of teaching emerge as a consequence of the brain principles. As we pointed out at the end of chapter 4, there are three elements. After each one, briefly note what it currently means to you.

1. **Relaxed alertness.**

    At a minimum, this state of mind requires low threat and high challenge on the part of both educators and students.

2. **Orchestrated immersion of the learner in multiple, complex, interactive experiences.**

    We must generate for learners experiences that approximate the sorts of experiences we all have as we acquire our native language.

3. **Active processing of experience.**

    This means engaging in the testing, reflective, and metacognitive processes that allow us to extract meaning from experience and solidify and expand new natural knowledge.

Activity

Review the brain principles with these three elements in mind. Which principles, either directly or indirectly, support the three elements we have identified? Why?

Note: The image in the felt meaning exercise is of a cow.

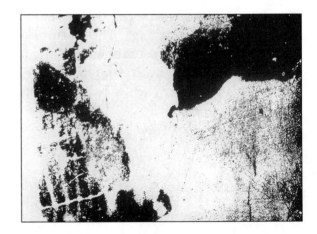

19

Relaxed Alertness

Remember that learning is enhanced by challenge and inhibited by threat. Thus, relaxed alertness is the combination of at least two important factors—low threat, or safety, and challenge. Remember that by threat we are referring to fear associated with a sense of helplessness. Anxiety or fear by itself does not necessarily induce a feeling of helplessness. Let us explore how to foster relaxed alertness in more depth.

Establishing a Sense of Safety within the School

Basics of a Learning Community

Our objective in brain-based instruction is for the school to become a learning community where there is respect for all and a degree of orderliness and taken-for-granted behaviors. One reason we emphasize the group process is that it begins to create the overall climate that is essential for individual students to feel relaxed alertness. This climate reveals itself in the entire school context.

Notes

Indicators and Questions: A Checklist

✔ Is the temperature acceptable?

✔ Does the setting, including architecture and layout, support both group work and private study?

✔ Is the environment "light" or depressing? What messages are being sent to children and adults?

✔ How much street noise is there? What sort of distraction is created by the intercom system?

✔ Is there artwork and other decoration? Does it include great works of art (in poster form)? Are students given the message that competence and quality are recognized and endorsed?

✔ What sort of group atmosphere is emerging? Are students helping each other with projects and concepts?

✔ Is there a way to introduce interesting places and changes in the physical environment? Is it done? Is technology used?

✔ Do teachers, administrators, and staff support each other? Are students aware of the actual organizational atmosphere?

✔ Is there any connection between course content (such as economics) and other school activities (such as fund-raising)?

✔ Do the school priorities reflect, in action, ostensible curriculum priorities? What value is placed on sports, socials, local politics, and educational goals?

✔ Is "school" happening inside and outside the classroom?

Establishing Intrinsic Motivation in Students

When students are intrinsically motivated they take charge of much of the learning. Even if test results are below expectations for a while, when you have evidence of self-directed and self-energized activity related to course content, your students are both open to and actively engaged in meaningful learning. The important point to note is that people can be "on task" in many different ways. For example, voluntarily returning to a project or problem is often much more of an indicator of ultimate success than dutifully doing busy work for a fixed length of time.

Useful Indicators of Intrinsic Motivation

- Is there clear evidence of student involvement, creativity, and enjoyment?

- Are there many different moods, including playfulness and serious thought?

- Are students asking questions or making observations that link content to life?

- Are their personal life themes, metaphors, interests, and dreams being engaged? For example, do students introduce course content into personal discussions and play in the class?

- Is there any sign of continuing motivation or student interest that expresses itself above and beyond the dictates of the class? Do students persevere with projects or return to them without reminders from the teacher? Are there any signs of positive collaboration? Does the collaboration continue after the lesson and after school?

- Are students dealing appropriately with dissonance? For example, do they persist to overcome difficulties in understanding or communication, or do they just give up at the first signs of difficulty?

- Do students suggest relevant projects of their own?

What Else Can We Do?

There are many strategies for directly assisting students to relax. The strategies include stretching, "best performance" visualizations, the use of appropriate music in the classroom, a set of routines for effectively beginning and ending classes or sessions, exercises in communication and active listening, the art of conflict resolution, and attention to rest and health.

We have included in appendix C a set of exercises that you can explore privately or in your study groups. Those that work well for you can then be introduced to help your students relax.

What most people find surprising is the fact that it is the teacher's state of mind that is critical. The happier and more relaxed you are, the more that attitude will be felt and absorbed by your students. The result is that you will be able to accomplish more with them and pay less attention to specific exercises that they need to practice.

Orderliness in a Learning Community

Reflect, for a moment, on the atmosphere in a range of different settings where creativity and respect for others flourish together—a museum, a theater, a high-performance research and development team.

Each of these has aspects of a set of features that adds vitality and strength to a learning community. We have extrapolated from them and other sources a set of features that together lead to what we call orderliness. When several of them come together, the safety, creativity, and effectiveness of the learning community are greatly enhanced.

This is not the time to seek to develop these features in depth. We simply invite you to reflect on the qualities that we list below. Our experience suggests that you may wish to adapt them to your classroom. This list, then, would provide direction for your next step in developing a learning community.

The key to real orderliness is to realize that it is not fragmented or limited to only certain procedures or guided by rules and punishment. Orderliness has to do with students and staff feeling connected and committed to a community that makes sense.

Activity

Look at the numbered items that follow the questions, and try to answer the questions for yourself or within your group.

- To what extent are these features in your school?

- To what extent would you like them to be features in your school?

- What can you do about it?

1. A sense of community

We have already discussed the importance of a safe and supportive community. It consists of a close-knit group of people who share some common goals and values and who have a built-in capacity to respect each other, even in the midst of profound disagreement.

2. A set of norms and guidelines

These behaviors are accepted and reinforced by everyone. Although they may be negotiated from time to time, the bottom line is that they guide some of the basic and everyday ways in which people behave. They may include such principles as being on time, listening without interrupting, respecting others' property, responding appropriately in specific places (for example, being quiet in parts of the library).

Some of these apply to everyone—adults and children. It is vital that they be modeled and lived by adults if they are to be respected and adhered to by children. Others apply to relations between adults and children. The point is that they are based on caring for and about people and the community. Children and adults feel connected by common values, goals, and ideas.

3. Routines

There is real power in routines that make sense and that are based on how human beings live. Routines operate in the office, in transport (for example, the way that buses work), in the ways in which classes change, in the time table, and elsewhere. The important element here is for everyone to adhere to agreed routines as much as possible, just to maintain the sense of rhythm in the way that things work.

4. Celebrations and special occasions

These bring life as well as order to a community. They mark special occasions, rites of passage, ways of beginning and ending, and specific and important moments. They are more than just routine activities. They need to be accompanied by a real felt sense of their importance.

5. Orderliness as a theme and idea

Underlying everything described above is the essence or idea of orderliness. The more we actually grasp this essence, the more relevant are our celebrations, routines, and so on. We need to explore the idea of orderliness as it operates in the real world. We are a part of it and it is a part of us.

6. Orderliness as an underlying curriculum theme

The global theme "order out of chaos" crosses every subject, skill, and discipline. History is a tale of order and disorder; the periodic table is the ordering of basic elements; social studies deals with multiple ways in which societies deal with order and disorder; math includes many ways of giving order to or perceiving order in the real world.

A result is that "order out of chaos" can be used as an ongoing or parallel theme in every course and class, even if it is only referred to occasionally. The more we explore it in the curriculum area, the better we grasp it. We therefore have an opportunity to relate the curriculum to the everyday life of the school because each is driven in part by the same general idea. Such a relationship helps students and educators to make more sense of the world of school.

7. Mutual respect

Orderliness emerges out of and contributes to mutual respect. The more we genuinely appreciate others for what they are, and the more they appreciate us, the stronger the community becomes, the easier it is to develop and implement basic rules and routines, and the more authenticity we find in celebrations and special occasions. Mutual respect among all people at all levels is a vital part of what binds a community together and makes orderliness possible.

20

Immersion of Learners in Complex Experiences

The brain is continuously making sense of experience. When we understand this deeply, we will begin to perceive that everything in the classroom is "experience." The presentation, the activity, the silent reading, the cooperative group, the work sheet—everything is being processed by the brain and is given a unique set of meanings. Is our classroom one in which students can see how learning is connected, and is it one in which compelling ideas clearly permeate everything that is learned? Or is our classroom one in which the fragmentary bits and pieces of facts and skills aimlessly add up, devoid of a sense of larger purpose and value?

Immersion in complex experiences means that the teaching experience is "rich," multilayered and complex enough so that there are many opportunities for students and teacher to use the language of the disciplines, ask and research critical questions, resolve opposing views and opinions, and engage in critical thinking and personal reflection.

Hobbies as Models

The way in which you master a hobby serves as an excellent example of what immersion looks like. Educators tend to think of learning in school as different from exploring a hobby, but much of genuine orchestration of complex experiences includes aspects reserved for sports or hobbies.

Activity

Elements that Are Often Present

Consider and make notes about your own hobby as we list some of the factors that may have been involved.

- A hobby is played out in a variety of different physical (space-time) contexts. It may be in a club, at home, out of state, or elsewhere.

- The discussion of our hobbies tends to include peers, those older or younger, and experts of all types.

- We tend to relate ongoing events and new information to our hobbies. In short, we are immersed in the subject.

- There tends to be informal conversation about our hobbies with friends and family members.

- There is usually some media coverage, even if we have to search for journals and TV programs prepared specifically for enthusiasts.

- Our hobbies tend to incorporate varying subject matter, from writing about something or communicating, to measuring and searching for significant patterns.

- Our hobbies naturally integrate many skills and subject areas.

- Doing research on and reading about our areas of interest are also natural. Hobbies create powerful networks of expert knowledge that the individual takes for granted but that make memory relatively easy. The networks can be tested easily. Let us assume the hobby is gardening. A brief announcement of a newly discovered fertilizer for prize flowers will be instantly remembered by the gardener. And even if the gardener doesn't remember the exact name of the product, the gist of the information will allow for a search (research) to proceed in some way.

- We may be exposed to direct instruction in classes or from experts.

- We will practice and rehearse skills and new
  vocabularies. (We have listed this last in order to
  put memorization and practice in a new perspective. It is the entirety of our experience that makes
  specific instruction interesting and practice
  appropriate.)

These are the types of processes that convert
information about our hobbies into natural knowledge.
We have expanded our understanding and expertise so
that the hobby is natural to us.

Activity

Elements that Must Be Continually Present

In addition to all the elements identified in the previous
activity, there are others that permeate our exploration of
a hobby. These are also critical to the orchestration of the
experiences that students need. Again, note the extent to
which these elements are present in your hobby.

- Evaluation and feedback. Whether directed by
  others or not, there is always some degree of
  assessment of competence and understanding in
  developing a hobby.

Thus, with brain-based instruction, learning is never
only for the test. Products, discussions, research, and
materials are evaluated on an ongoing basis. Students
make their own goals and check their own achievement,
peers evaluate and make suggestions, and teachers have
suggestions and input. Final products, demonstrations, or
exhibits can be evaluated by a number of people drawn
from the mentioned zones.

- Natural use of the language of the disciplines. Everyone from neophytes to experts continually uses the language of the hobby in interactions.

One aspect of immersion, therefore, is the continual use of new and unfamiliar vocabulary and concepts through natural interaction driven by projects and other orchestrated experiences.

- Ongoing student interest. The interest of an enthusiast is constant.

Similarly, the subject and questions raised should be of interest to students. Whenever possible, students should generate the necessary questions and plan the research. Teachers need to monitor the interest level and ensure that experiences are genuinely meaningful and of consequence in the world beyond the classroom.

Commentary

Orchestrating the immersion of learners in complex experiences takes time to learn and can be a very sophisticated process. Ultimately, the teacher must rely on student interest, outside support, and help from all kinds of enrichment materials such as primary sources and local exhibits and museums, computer software, and community experts.

Fortunately, there is a great deal of material and information available to us. The key is to grasp the underlying objective and principles so that we can utilize materials in the most effective way.

There is a great deal of talk these days about saving the environment. We must, for the environment sustains our bodies. But as humans we also require support for our spirits, and this is what certain kinds of place provide. The catalyst that converts any physical location—any environment if you will—into a place, is the process of experiencing deeply.

— Alan Gussow in *The Earth Speaks*

21

The Active Processing of Experience

By itself, experience is not enough. It must be constantly reviewed, recognized, articulated, and consolidated. Immersion provides the complex experience, and relaxed alertness ensures that students are safe to experiment and challenge themselves. Active processing makes certain that the content is meaningful, learned, and deeply understood.

How many of us, for instance, have been "tested" as new teachers, entering a classroom for the first time? How often have you observed a child trying out a word or phrase to see what it means and to find out what sort of reaction it will elicit? And even when a young baby is exploring—moving around a room and pushing things to see if they will move—he or she is testing, comparing, contrasting, trying things out, and generally fitting things together in ways that make sense.

At a more sophisticated level, we formalize this testing process and it becomes the scientific method. Thus, hypotheses are tested and examined, and we end up with the belief that some theories are sound and others are weak.

This entire realm of exploration and analysis is what we mean by active processing. Thus, active processing is the consolidation and internalization of information and procedures by the learner, in a way that is both personally meaningful and conceptually coherent.

Experts and professionals always process experience:

- Lawyers ask critical questions.

- Doctors rely on keen observation and diagnosis.

- Architects must relate form to function.

- Therapists look and listen for hidden meanings.

- Coaches monitor skill, performance, and attitude.

Active processing, then, is the key to perceiving patterns and making sense of experience. In this chapter we simply introduce a set of ideas and processes that you might like to consider and test for yourself. They will prove surprisingly powerful in the long term.

Some Ways to Help Students Process Experience

Begin to explore the following list by recalling some time in your life when you used such processes.

1. **Concretize basic categories and patterns.**
   Describe how it looks, sounds, feels.
   What is familiar? What is unfamiliar?
   Describe the smallest details.
   Describe the largest patterns.
   Identify the context.

2. **Rehearse creatively.**
   Repetition in rounds and in groups
   Games
   Puzzles
   Songs
   Exaggerated imitation and modeling
   Visualization

3. **Relate to personal experience and what is already known.**

   What do I already know about it?

   What does it remind me of?

   Is it bigger? smaller? faster? slower? and so on.

   Where else does it occur?

   Do I know others who know something about it?

4. **Explore the story.**

   What do you think happened here?

   Who or what was involved?

   Describe the physical setting.

   When did it all happen?

   What else do you think might happen?

   Who or what else might be involved?

5. **Identify main themes and ideas.**

   Is there an abstract concept that this is all about?

   What makes you think that a particular theme is involved?

   What other ideas or themes are being worked out?

   Discuss other contexts in which these themes play a part.

   Are there any central metaphors or analogies?

6. **Use the Socratic method to test thinking.**

   Specify what, where, who, how, when.

   What are the basic categories? Analyze their features.

   Compare and contrast categories.

   What are the hidden and obvious assumptions? What is being taken for granted?

   What specific inferences are being made? Are there other conclusions?

   Are there counterexamples?

7. **Make general observations.**

   Develop a hypothesis.

   Decide how to test it.

   Decide what evidence would be needed.

   Conduct the test and formulate conclusions.

   Discuss and analyze, using critical thinking, the Socratic method.

8. **Explore aesthetics.**

   Is this beautiful? elegant? harmonious? Why?

   What principles and criteria are involved?

   Discuss different values and perspectives.

   Discuss the relationship between beauty and effectiveness.

9. **Generate alternatives.**

   Find new analogies and metaphors.

   Turn ideas and procedures upside down, back to front, and inside out.

   Call on imagination, adventure, intuition, and play.

   How would other cultures or roles interpret this?

10. **Analyze feelings.**

    What do I want to do?

    What did I do?

    How did it work out?

    What could I have done differently?

    What do my feelings and impressions tell me about this?

Commentary

Much of what is written here should be familiar. It is the underlying purpose for employing these procedures that is significant. These are all ways to generate and elicit meaning from experience. Hence, they can all be used in connection with **any** subject matter. In fact, active processing becomes a superb way to generate interdisciplinary teaching naturally.

You should note that orchestrated immersion, relaxed alertness, and active processing are not used in a linear way. They are interactive and each contains some aspects of the others. Remember also that they apply to the learning of everyone—administrators, teachers, support staff, and students. Putting it all together takes time and is very challenging.

Suggestions

- Adjust to the level of your students (but keep it challenging!).

- Be prepared to model active processing in your interactions with students personally and in their interactions with each other.

- Make active processing (and its companion, reflection) real by taking it into all aspects of students' lives.

- Use active processing everywhere.

Our final suggestion is that you explore and practice active processing in your study groups once the rest of *MindShifts* has been processed. It will prove to be a powerful tool for further developing your learning community.

A Final Word

As we mentioned at the beginning, this is not a "how-to" book. Our objective is for people to appreciate so deeply the nature of learning and teaching that they begin to make any necessary changes inside themselves. The techniques and procedures in this book are intended to assist that change.

As understanding deepens, we naturally become more capable of designing new procedures for our classes. We begin to see more of what has to be dealt with. Our sense of rhythm and timing and context improve.

All of these changes take time and inevitably involve some personal questioning and occasional doubt. They are indispensable aspects of meaningful learning and are to be welcomed and not feared.

However, there is no point in having each of us reinvent the wheel. It is valuable to discover what others do and recommend. For those reasons we suggest that you make use of programs that others have developed and that you compare notes with one another. We are also compiling a series of additional books, each of which explores in depth an aspect of teaching for the expansion of natural knowledge. These will combine some very powerful techniques and procedures with more reflection and self-inventory.

We look forward to sharing these books with you. We also welcome your comments and suggestions. Feel free to write to us in care of Caine Learning, P.O. Box 1847, Idyllwild, CA 92549.

Appendix A

The Process for Ordered Sharing in Groups

1. **The group sits in a closed circle.**

2. **Agree upon your core material to read or explore.**

   Ideally it will be brief and profound. One example is a selection from a book of sayings or quotations. Some verse from Walt Whitman is another example. A third example is a poster of a great work of art. In chapter 5, we suggested that you use one of the "big ideas" with which each chapter on the brain principles begins. Following are some examples:

   Everything is connected.

   The whole is greater than the sum of the parts.

3. **Examine the material.**

   The text could be read aloud. The poster can be observed. When you use a principle, the whole group could recite it together.

4. **Share opinions.**

   One person expresses a personal opinion about the chosen subject, with a time limit of perhaps one or two minutes.

   The person on the left expresses an opinion next.

   Sharing continues around the circle.

   The direction around the circle does not matter. What does matter is that there is no competition for time. This process is ordered, and each person shares in turn. You will know exactly when it is your turn.

5. **No one makes any comment whatsoever about what another says.**

   There is no opposition, nor is there verbal support. However, every silent member pays full attention to what is being said. During these times what is encouraged is expression of personal opinion and the giving of permission to others to hold and express their opinions.

6. **The group leader for the meeting monitors timing and participation.**

   If someone exceeds the agreed upon time, simply say "time" or "process," or use some other signal to indicate that time is up. The person who is talking stops immediately. She or he does not continue to complete the thought.

7. **As a variation, the group leader can make two interventions: She or he can encourage people who talk very loudly to modulate their voice and encourage people who talk very softly to speak up.**

8. **Everyone reflects in silence upon what was said and upon her or his own reactions to the content and the process.**

9. **For advanced groups, open discussion can then follow. It should never be focused on arguing with or correcting a participant.**

   You can talk about the different points of view that were expressed and what you learned. You could also talk about how you felt during the process itself. Was it easy or difficult to hold your tongue? How does the atmosphere in a group change when people are not competing for time to talk? Does the process shed any light on the nature of orderliness and the learning community? Note that you can discuss the same or similar questions every week. If you do, note whether your observations and opinions change. You might also like to reflect each week on whether this process is having any long-term effect.

Commentary

At the heart of learning is the capacity to be open to genuine change. In addition to hearing other points of view, we need to be able to generate the mind state of active uncertainty and the group atmosphere of respectful support. This technique may prove deeply frustrating, particularly to those who like to interrupt or who have very strong opinions. Hence, it needs to be experienced many different times.

We do not suggest running an entire session or class like this, though some may wish to do so. We do suggest that this procedure be regularly included in your group sessions.

We suggest that you stick to the procedure quite rigorously for a little while, and then modify it as you see fit. You will also find that this can serve as a model for some areas of administration and teaching. It also becomes a way to gain further insight into many other strategies that you may use, ranging from cooperative learning to conflict resolution.

Appendix B

Perceptual Styles

The following descriptors are Geoffrey and Renate Caine's synthesis of many learning and social style instruments commercially available. We use them as guidelines for grasping the various ways in which people perceive their worlds. We have labeled these perceptual styles Nurturer, Evaluator, Director, and Adventurer.

Commentary

There are many ways of exploring individual differences and similarities. For example, cultural background is important. Responses also vary when we are distressed and when we are relaxed. However, these style differences are very useful in providing insight into how you and others communicate, relate, respond, learn, and teach. There is no limit to the contexts in which they can be explored and applied.

It is important not to overemphasize styles, of course. We all have aspects of all styles and often *need* to develop the areas in which we are weak, rather than just retreat into areas where we are strong. Thus, the goal must be to immerse yourself and your students in a wide range of experiences and a richly integrated and complex environment that is both safe and challenging. This goal automatically provides support and exposure for all styles to some extent.

Remember also the power of context and culture. It is possible that some contexts, by design or belief system, favor certain styles. Hence, there is always more to learn about how we communicate.

Everyone has aspects of all four styles. However, one style is usually dominant. Try to find the one that describes best how you tend to see your world and the people in it.

NURTURER

People who are primarily nurturers tend to have many of the following characteristics.

Personal

Being close to people is extremely important to you. So is working with your hands. You have intense feelings of loyalty, and friends are central to your happiness. You need people around you and can become depressed and morose when people are not around in your life. Because you care so much, you like to help others. You work hard for causes that you believe in. Your desire to work hard means that you can also be used by others, because you are anxious to please them. You may end up giving too much and then feeling hurt and resentful.

You need to take time out to determine what your values are, because your sense of loyalty and compassion for others may lead you to put your own thoughts and feelings aside when someone else feels differently. Remember that your feelings are your way of "knowing," and you want to capitalize on this knowing as a strength. As an adolescent, you needed to figure out what you wanted to do before you entered into any long-term relationship. You are capable of giving and giving until one day you need to leave the situation and can't explain why to yourself or the other(s). You'll have given too much too often while you weren't aware of what was happening.

You like to touch and feel the world around you and often need to do that before you fully understand what is happening. You also like to make contact and to be intimate. People with styles different from yours may feel that you are intruding because you get too close too often. You also tend to sense feelings and then hunt for words to express them. You can be very sensitive and bright, but it takes you more time to think than others, because along with information you need to scan and incorporate your feelings. However, you should explore when to trust your inner feelings, because when you are free to take time without pleasing or protecting another, you often turn out to be right.

Work

You tend to need details and get frustrated if you don't get enough instructions or the time to "do it right." You prefer a lot of help and reassurance to make sure you are doing things correctly and if such reassurance was not given early in your schooling (a teacher was impatient or others could do things much faster), you may have decided that you were not a good learner. If you did have the right kind of attention and help, however, you might be quite intellectual because of your love of detail.

You need personal contact with your administrator, so the best administrators for you tend to be the ones who care about people in general. Since feelings are so important to you, working only for an outcome or a product is often not enough, and critical or negative comments can hurt you deeply. Reward for you means someone cares and has taken time to notice and recognize what you have done.

Because touch helps you understand, you should find ways to explore physically any subject. Use clay, models, and movement to learn anything from learning theory to computing. In learning, your first need is to feel at home with the subject.

Things to Avoid

Above all, avoid getting involved with negative people or people who are simply not good for you. You need to spend much of your time in the company of people who care about people, individuals who really allow you to be you, whether you are happy or angry or slow or analytical.

When you don't get what you want or when you downshift, you tend to manipulate people by making them feel guilty and through self pity ("poor me"). Try to develop a sense of your own worth and focus on taking action. Doing so will allow you to face negative situations without feeling helpless.

Things to Do for Yourself

Spend time by yourself and *think* things through or find a close friend and talk things through. Making your own decisions can be tough for you because you need people so much that you are tempted to compromise. You need to separate you from how others feel about something.

Learn to forgive and forget, develop a positive attitude, and develop your own interests and ideas. Find a hobby or interest that is creative and physical. Also find a project of which you are the leader. Remember that you can learn from criticism. Try to separate what is useful from what is not.

A good axiom for you is to remember Ivan Barzakov's 3**A** principles (1988):

Acknowledge what is happening.

Accept the world as it is.

Act on what is needed and what you can actually do.

Follow through on the third "A."

EVALUATOR

People who are primarily evaluators tend to have many of the following characteristics.

Personal

Order and system are very important to you. How things "look," either in the real world or in your mind, is also important. When you are creative, you have a very good sense of design. Your first impression of a person or place is based on what you see rather than on a conversation. For example, how people dress, the style and color combinations or clothes, may be something you notice. You can see the beauty in the world around you and are attracted by elegant design.

You also care what other people think of you and how you look to them. You love events and things to be well ordered and to have a beginning, a middle, and an end. You are systematic and a good planner and you like things to take place according to your plans. The result is that you have expectations about how things will turn out. That means that you can also be inflexible and may find it difficult to adjust when something unexpected happens. You can also be a perfectionist who won't be happy until everything is "picture perfect." You may also be overly critical, which can stop you from enjoying life as much as you could.

When faced with a decision, you like to have the reasons for both sides and to think things through. You have the ability to see both sides of a question, and you like to have time to make up your mind. Because you see all the possibilities and the problems, at times you tend to "sit on the fence" before acting. However, once you form an opinion you tend to stick to it firmly.

You are naturally neat and orderly and like things to "look right." If you are angry at the world or when you have some of the adventurer in you, you can dress in unique, dramatic, or even bizarre ways. Whatever your statement to the world, it will be made with something people can "see."

Work

You like to do things right and to pay attention to appearance, method, design, and detail. You need a lot of recognition and time to create your vision. If the time was denied you as a child, you may have become discouraged and rebelled by doing a sloppy job (if you can't achieve the best, why try?) or dressing in sloppy ways. It can be hard for an evaluator to find the middle way. Either something has to look perfect, and you stay up all night to make it so, or you don't care and do relatively little.

An evaluator is a student teachers often like because, when he or she cares, an evaluator will make whatever he or she does look good. Evaluators like administrators and colleagues who give them diagrams and pictures. It would help you to practice drawing and design and to create word pictures through writing and theater. You also need to take time to see how things fit together. You often have visions, pictures, or dreams that other people don't see, and a good leader for you is one who helps you to express those pictures and ideas.

Things to Avoid

Acknowledge your first impressions, but take the time to look below the surface, because things are not always what they seem. Because you may procrastinate, give yourself deadlines. You should also avoid waiting for everything to be perfect before you begin a project. The key is do something—take some action—and then evaluate it.

When disappointed, angry, hurt, or overwhelmed, you tend to withdraw from people. This withdrawal is important and appropriate for you, but help others to understand that you need to do this, and *don't* withdraw too much or too long. You could lose friends, and some people will resent you for "leaving" them.

Things to Do for Yourself

Give yourself lots of time to plan and complete projects, provided you also give yourself deadlines. You need time to make things look the way you want. In addition, make sure that you regularly *act* instead of just thinking.

Try to develop compassion so you are not so hard on yourself and others. People have become what they are because of the experiences that shaped them. When you learn to accept people for what and who they are, you will also relax your judgment about yourself and others and be happier.

You are very creative and artistic and need to find a way to express your artistic and creative ideas visually.

DIRECTOR

People who are primarily directors tend to have many of the following characteristics.

Personal

Challenge and leadership are both extremely important to you, and you like to have and give direction. You tend to make decisions quickly and stick to them. You want the facts before making any decision, but you tend to be impatient with detail and look for the big picture. It is important to you to understand what is happening and how things work. Words and sounds are very important to you, and you tend to take seriously what someone says. You are good at discerning when people do not mean what they say, and you do not like those people at all. You do, however, collect information and use it.

You love a big challenge and easily put pressure on others even if you hate being under pressure yourself. You tend to be a leader, but you may alienate people by seeming not to care about them or being too sharp or abrupt. An organized plan is important to you. You tend to plan big and finish what you start. If someone or something stops you from developing projects and succeeding at them, you can become very depressed or angry. You don't like to waste time and can be blunt and even rude at times. You do not like people who talk about their feelings or don't "stand up" to you, but you will probably fight if confronted or attacked.

Work

You tend to benefit more than most from a lecture given by someone you respect or about something that interests you, because you like to learn by listening. You have a strong need for accomplishments and challenge, and work needs to provide you with these. You can become very impatient with yourself and others, particularly if you have misjudged the time it takes to complete a task, and you tend not to want to hear other people's excuses. Words and sounds are important to you, and you should learn to use them. You do well with people who stick to the facts and help you see how things work and do not expect you to share personal feelings. In work, you will probably end up in a leadership position, because that seems most comfortable to you and allows you to supervise your plans while they become real. You like to talk ideas out, but without taking much time.

Things to Avoid

Avoid being too "bossy" and working with too many projects that require attention to a great deal of detail. Don't put yourself under pressure, and if you delegate, remember that others do not necessarily like or handle pressure any better. Avoid becoming dogmatic about issues, and don't feel you have to prove so much. You may question the authority of others without thinking it through first. Try not to tell people what they should do with their lives. Beware of your tendency to fight when confronted. There are often other options and solutions.

Things to Do for Yourself

You need projects where you can take charge and that have a good chance of succeeding. Practice being realistic about how much you can accomplish within the time available. It may help to learn to play a musical instrument or a sport that gives you a good sense of rhythm and timing. You need to work at relaxing and taking the time to understand how other people feel and why feelings are important. In order to be a real leader, you will need compassion so that you are able to understand what someone else is experiencing. Your own feelings are also important, and addressing them will help you become a truly good leader who balances facts with values and human emotions. Remember also that the words people use to describe something are not as concrete as they sound to you. Honoring your word is very important, but you need to see that many people use language hypothetically or metaphorically. For them words are less important.

ADVENTURER

People who are primarily adventurers tend to have many of the following characteristics.

Personal

Change and variety are very important to you, including a variety of sensory experience. You are probably best known for your ability to anticipate what is going to happen in the future. Sometimes, however, you just guess. You live in a world of possibilities, and you are willing to look at things that are unique. You don't mind unique authority. You tend not to take authority, be that rules or people, as infallible. To you there is always another way, and if rules or people don't make sense to you, you are capable of ignoring them and developing your own. The risk is that you lose a sense of orderliness and respect for other people's perspectives and needs.

You love sensation, variety, and fun and often find yourself involved in several projects and ideas at the same time. In fact, you can spread yourself too thin. You may also put off completing projects because you feel that you know how they will turn out, and you lose interest. You tend to be a risk taker because the new usually seems more interesting to you. You are the kind of person a friend can wake up at three in the morning for an emergency and you'll think it's great because it's a change. You can be a good friend and really enjoy people. You are often popular because you love to entertain and "play around." You listen to others and tend to know what they want and need and don't mind giving it to them if it doesn't restrict you or bore you to do so. You can, however, change your mind or "forget" promises or appointments because something else more interesting came up. When in balance, you are a very good leader because of your ability to keep in touch with all facets of a project and find solutions to problems.

Work

You tend to decide more by intuition than by analysis, which means that you often come up with the right answer but don't always know how you did it. You tend to be a good problem solver because you believe in the possibility of an answer and don't hesitate to think of solving a problem in a new and unique way. Teachers tended to see you as an underachiever because you could arrive at the right answer and improve on what others did but could not always explain your answer or repeat your performance when called on to do so. As a result, your grades did not reflect what your teachers saw you as capable of doing. You may not handle details very well, and you need self-discipline.

You may be very impatient with ordinary classroom teaching and regular meetings, especially those that deal with the status quo and appear to stall your interactive bent. Lack of variety and challenge probably brought out the clown in you as a student, and you could be disruptive in any situation if you were bored or not committed. You really need to challenge yourself. Remember not to spread yourself too thin and sign up for too many things. You need much of your work to be in a context where you are permitted to do things in a new and unique way, are challenged to do your best, and are allowed to solve problems in your own way. Also, even though it seems counterintuitive, work in very quiet, almost peaceful surroundings. As long as the world is challenging, you may find that you actually concentrate better and are more productive in a peaceful setting.

Things to Avoid

Try to stay with one thing until it is finished or put things back before you go on to another project. This may be hard for you but is absolutely necessary if you don't want to waste your talents. It is critical that you challenge yourself and go beyond what is expected as a minimum effort.

Remember that not everyone is so ready to look at a new idea or ignore conventional rules and authority. Also remember that there are real limits. When you run into trouble, you are capable of escaping reality by looking at a world of all possibilities without restrictions. This practice is not very productive. You can fool yourself into thinking you can do anything you choose. You are then shocked by very real barriers that prevent you from implementing your path of choice. You can be casual and intuitive but shocked that the real world expects you to be able to pay close attention to details.

Try not to exaggerate things or be too emotionally dramatic. Other people don't know how to handle such drama and can get terribly upset, even though you actually feel that the dramatic expression is natural for emphasis. You may find yourself surprised if other people leave or stay away because they have been overwhelmed by you.

Things to Do for Yourself

Learn to relax, slow down, and turn your mind off. Doing so will allow you to see things more clearly. Make sure you develop your interests and talents and produce a product that you can be proud of or that is recognized by peers.

Develop patience with others who do not share your ability to see how things could, instead of should, be done. Keep your commitments instead of letting the current mood carry you, and get involved in a project that helps you complete things, respect other people, and acknowledge their contributions and ideas.

Note: A perceptual styles instrument and a set of exercises for educators to use with their students will soon be available. Contact Caine Learning at (909) 659-0152.

Appendix C

Additional Exercises

These techniques and procedures serve two ends. First, they will help you to develop a deeper appreciation of how the brain learns, in part through the experience that you have as you use the technique and in part as a consequence of your own reflections and discussions about your experience. One way to approach this procedure is to explore a different technique in each of your weekly group meetings and then to practice every day for the next week.

Second, as you master the techniques, they will become extremely useful in your classroom teaching. The point to remember is that you do need to become proficient, and you also need to ensure that you use the techniques and procedures in a way that suits your style and context.

You will also find that you will want to amend and improve them in your own ways. We therefore recommend that you add your own insights and comments on the pages provided.

Meditation

These techniques are intended to lead to generally improved mental and physical well-being. For instance, as explained in *Making Connections,* meditation reduces the presence of debilitating hormones that impede health and clarity of thinking. The techniques are devoid of indoctrination or bias. They are important because they are procedures that rest the mind and the physiology.

Good relaxation has these benefits:

1. **It is the best nonmedicinal cure for blood pressure irregularities.**

2. **It helps to regulate sleep.**

3. **It improves general health.**

4. **It enhances creativity.**

Relaxation operates in two different ways. First, the procedure itself is gentle but effective. Second, because it is repeated every day, it helps to develop a sense of order and rhythm.

These techniques are most effective when done for twenty minutes twice a day, preferably before a meal (such as before breakfast and dinner).

Breath Meditation

Step 1   Lie down or sit comfortably.

Step 2   Observe your chest move as you breathe.

Step 3   Have someone count slowly to four, and breathe in as she or he counts. Then have the person count backward; breathe out as she or he counts. Observe your chest move as you breathe. Do this four or five times.

Step 4   Keep breathing on your own to a slow count, observing your chest.

Step 5   After a few minutes, observe the flow of your breath rather than your chest. Perhaps attend just to the inflow and outflow for about five to ten minutes.

Step 6   When you have finished, stretch your whole body while sitting or lying down.

Note: **The breathing tends to be very relaxing, and you may fall asleep. That is okay.**

Step 7   Ground yourself. Look around you and notice some very basic, ordinary details. How high is the ceiling? What color is the carpet? What is the weather like? What are you going to do next?

Step 8   Get up slowly, and do not do any heavy exercise for a little while.

Word Meditation

Step 1   Select a stimulus word by combining two syllables, examples of which are in the list of sounds that follow. Any meaningless sound will do.

Step 2   Find a quiet, comfortable place where you can sit without interruption for twenty minutes.

Step 3   Loosen your clothes. Place both feet on the floor. Rest your hands comfortably in your lap.

Step 4   Breathe deeply two or three times.

Step 5   Sit quietly and observe the random thoughts that come into your mind. Notice how natural and light those thoughts are.

Step 6   With the same degree of gentleness and lightness, repeat your word silently. *Never* concentrate hard on saying it or getting it right.

Step 7   You will find other thoughts and feelings coming to mind, which is quite natural. As you become aware that your mind has wandered, simply return to your word.

Step 8   Either open your eyes gently to look at your watch in order to check the time, or use some very gentle alarm to let you know that twenty minutes has elapsed.

Step 9   Stop saying the word, and begin to breathe more deeply, keeping your eyes closed.

Step 10 Open your eyes very gently and easily after a minute or so.

Step 11 Stay seated and relax for another few minutes.

Step 12 Do not meditate right after eating or before going to sleep.

Step 13 Do not exercise immediately after meditation.

Examples of sounds to choose from

NIYOM	QAYAM	PAHUM	GAJOM	SOJOM
HAJIM	WAYUM	REHIM	KOYUM	VOYAM
PEFIM	NALUM	VAJIM	REGOM	WOJIM

These are only examples. You might want to invent other words to use.

Suggestions and Possible Experiences

- As you relax, you begin to become aware of feelings or thoughts that you have been having and that might have been hidden. These can vary a great deal.

- Temporary feelings of depression, joy, and nothing much happening at all are all common.

- It is also quite common to twitch and to have some strange thoughts. Some people see light or colors.

Note: For these three, just observe your experience, and gently return to your word or your breathing.

- Pressure on the forehead is common. Don't persevere or strain with the meditation. Just relax.

- A good general rule is that if you feel undue discomfort, just stop. However, you should then find a substitute activity that gives you the opportunity to work through any beliefs or "unfinished business" that leads to your being disturbed.

- It is okay to fall asleep. If you have time, just finish your meditation afterward.

Focusing

Focusing is not concentrating. It is a matter of being attentive to an object or event or thought. The difference between concentrating and focusing lies in the degree of effort involved. Focusing requires much less effort and is thoughtlike in quality. If we close our eyes and watch thoughts come and go, the effortlessness with which unselected thoughts appear gives an idea of how focusing feels.

This exercise is excellent for building awareness and for increasing understanding by penetrating the meaning of a thought or feeling.

Phase 1

Practice the breathing meditation described above.

Phase 2

The key is to place the thought or feeling in your awareness and focus on it in the same way as you focus on your breathing or as you use contemplation in the exercise on page 247. It is *not* a matter of thinking or analyzing.

Rather, it is a matter of allowing a relaxed mind to explore an issue in its own way.

Examples of issues to focus on include

A personal relationship

Computing

The nature of learning

Each of the brain principles

Sometimes nothing will happen. Sometimes you will have quite profound insights. In any event, focusing takes time. Mastery, here, lies in not concentrating and not using effort. Focusing is a great character builder because it can develop persistence and the ability to pursue and investigate something in depth.

Critical Thinking

One of the best ways to help a person grasp the hidden depth in any subject or experience is to help her or him ask good questions about it. That is why critical thinking needs to be experienced as part of, and embedded in, every subject in the curriculum. In fact this is simply a condensed version of some aspects of active processing.

Following are some questions to ask about any subject or process, including the material in this workbook:

What, specifically, is being said or argued?

What does it remind me of?

What evidence do I have for that position?

What are the hidden assumptions?

Who stands to gain, and what?

Are there other points of view?

How would I justify an alternative point of view?

Is there any other subject or procedure like this? In what way?

Does it confirm or disconfirm what is being said?

What do I need to do to gain more understanding?

References

Allport, S. 1986. *Explorer of the Black Box: The Search for the Cellular Basis of Memory.* New York: W. W. Norton.

Altweger, B., C. Edelsky, and B. Flores. 1987. "Whole Language: What's New?" *The Reading Teacher* 41, no. 2:144–54.

Amabile, T. 1989. *Growing up Creative.* New York: Crown.

Barzakov, I. 14 July 1988. Unpublished notes from the Optimalearning™ Workshop.

Bateson, G. 1972. *Steps to an Ecology of Mind.* Aronson.

Bransford, D., and M. Johnson. 1972. "Contextual Prerequisites for Understanding: Some Investigations of Comprehensive Recall." *Journal of Verbal Learning and Verbal Behavior* 11:717–21.

Caine, G., and R. N. Caine. 1991. "Downshifting: A Hidden Condition that Sabotages Change." *The Instructional Leader* (May).

Caine, R. N., and G. Caine. 1994. *Making Connections: Teaching and the Human Brain.* Menlo Part, Calif.: Addison-Wesley.

Campbell, J. 1989. *The Improbable Machine.* New York: Simon and Schuster.

Combs, A. W., and D. Snygg. 1959. *Individual Behavior: A Perceptual Approach to Behavior.* New York: Harper and Row.

Cousins, N. 1989. *Head First: The Biology of Hope.* New York: E.P. Dutton.

Diamond, M. C. 1985. *Brain Growth in Response to Experience.* Seminar, University of California, Riverside, March 23, 1985.

Gazzaniga, M. 1985. *The Social Brain: Discovering the Networks of the Mind.* New York: Basic Books.

Gibran, K. 1966. *The Prophet.* London: Heinemann.

Goodman, K. 1986. *What's Whole in Whole Language?* Portsmouth, N.H.: Heinemann.

Halgren, E., C. L. Wilson, N. K. Squires, J. Engel, R. D. Walter, and P. H. Crandall. 1983. "Dynamics of the Hippocampal Contribution to Memory: Stimulation and Recording Studies in Humans." In *Molecular, Cellular and Behavioral Neurobiology of the Hippocampus,* edited by W. Seifert. New York: Academic Press.

Halpern, D. 1989. *Thought and Knowledge: An Introduction to Critical Thinking.* Hillsdale, N.J.: Lawrence Erlbaum and Assoc.

Hand, J. D. 1984. "Split Brain Theory and Recent Results in Brain Research: Implications for the Design of Instruction." In *Instructional Development: The State of the Art, II,* edited by R. K. Bass and C. R. Dills. Dubuque, Iowa: Kendall/Hunt.

Hart, L. A. 1975. *How the Brain Works: A New Understanding of Human Learning, Emotion, and Thinking.* New York: Basic Books.

———. 1983. *Human Brain, Human Learning.* New York: Longman.

Hayard, S. 1984. *A Guide for the Advanced Soul.* Avalon, Aust.: In-Tune Books.

Heider, J. 1985. *The Tao of Leadership.* New York: Bantam.

Helprin, M. 1975. *A Jew of Persia in* A Dove of the East. San Diego: Harcourt Brace Jovanovich.

Hunter, M. 1990. Preface to *Changing School through Staff Development: 1990 Yearbook of the Association for Supervision and Curriculum Development,* edited by B. Joyce. Alexandria, Va: ASCD.

Jacobs, W. J., and L. Nadel. 1985. "Stress-Induced Recovery of Fears and Phobias." *Psychological Review* 92, no. 4:512–31

Joyce, B., J. Wolf, and E. Calhoun. 1993. *The Self-Renewing School.* Virginia: ASCD.

Kovalik, S. 1989. *Teachers Make the Difference—with Integrated Thematic Instruction.* Oak Creek, Ariz.: Susan Kovalik.

Lakoff, G. 1987. *Women, Fire, and Dangerous Things.* Chicago: University of Chicago Press.

Lakoff, G., and M. Johnson. 1980. *Metaphors We Live By.* Chicago: Chicago University Press.

Langer, E. J. 1989. *Mindfulness.* Massachusetts: Addison-Wesley.

Levy, B. 1972. "Do Teachers Sell Girls Short?" *Today's Education* 61:27–29.

Lozanov, G. 1978. *Suggestology and Outlines of Suggestopedy.* New York: Gordon and Breach.

McGuinness, D., and K. Pribram. 1980. "The Neuropsychology of Attention: Emotional and Motivational Controls." In *The Brain and Psychology,* edited by M. D. Wittrock. New York: Academic Press.

Nadel, L., and J. Wilmer. 1980. "Context and Conditioning: A Place for Space. *Physiological Psychology* 8:218–28.

Nadel, L., J. Wilmer, and E. M. Kurz. 1984. "Cognitive Maps and Environmental Context." Chapter 8 in *Context and Learning,* edited by P. Balsam and A. Tomi. Hillsdale, N.J.: Lawrence Erlbaum.

Nummela, R., and T. Rosengren. 1986. "The Brain's Routes and Maps: Vital Connections in Learning." *NAASP Bulletin: The Journal for Middle Level and High School Administrators* 72:83–86.

O'Keefe, J., and L. Nadel. 1978. *The Hippocampus as a Cognitive Map.* New York: Oxford University Press.

Ornstein, R., and D. Sobel. 1987. *The Healing Brain: Breakthrough Discoveries about How the Brain Keeps Us Healthy.* New York: Simon and Schuster.

Rosenfield, I. 1988. *The Invention of Memory.* New York: Basic Books.

Senge, P. M. 1990. *The Fifth Discipline: The Art and Practice of the Learning Organization.* New York: Doubleday.

Shalley, C. 1988. *Humanities Program, Hightstown High School: Curriculum for the Integrated Humanities Program at Hightstown High School, Hightstown, N.J.* Unpublished manuscript.

Smith, F. 1986. *Insult to Intelligence: The Bureaucratic Invasions of Our Classrooms.* Portsmouth, N.H.: Heinemann Educational Books.

Springer, S., and G. Deutsch. 1985. *Left Brain, Right Brain.* 2d ed. New York: W. H. Freeman.

Van Matre, S., and B. Weiler. 1983. *The Earth Speaks.* Illinois: The Institute for Earth Education.

Vygotsky, L. S. 1978. *Mind in Society.* Cambridge, Mass.: Harvard University Press.

Wheatley, M. J. 1992. *Leadership and the New Science.* San Francisco: Berrett-Koehler.

Whitman, W. 1958. "Song of the Open Road." In *Leaves of Grass.* New York: Signet.

Index

Use "BIG IDEAS" to focus on the Big Picture of teaching and learning

★ ★

Redesign your 'mental models' with the MindShifts process for group change!

MINDSHIFTS
Windows to the Mind, vol. 4
by Renate Nummela Caine, Ph.D., Geoffrey Caine, LL.M., and Sam Crowell, Ed.D.

Staff Development

Here's the how-to video you need to help bring meaningful change to your school. Watch this video to see MindShifts process groups in action and discover the need for educators to transform their thinking collectively. Enhance your personal and professional development with this video and accompanying discussion guide, or study it as a complement to the *MindShifts* text you are already using.

60-minute, full-color, VHS video. 27-page discussion guide.
1708-W . . . $149

★ ★

SPECIAL OFFER!
SAVE $50!

Order Windows to the Mind vol. 3 and 4 and SAVE 50!

1712-W . . . $248

- -

ORDER FORM ☎ Please include your phone number in case we have questions about your order.

Qty.	Item #	Title	Unit Price	Total
	1821-W	MindShifts Posters (set of 12)	$29	
	1082-W	The Re-Enchantment of Learning	$29	
	1707-W	Windows to the Mind, Vol. 3	$149	
	1708-W	Windows to the Mind, Vol. 4	$149	
	1712-W	Windows to the Mind, Vols. 3 & 4 (Special Offer)	$248	

Name _____

Address _____

City _____

State _____ Zip _____

Phone (_____) _____

E-mail _____

100%
SATISFACTION GUARANTEE

Remember, if you are not entirely satisfied just return the products in saleable condition within 90 days and get a full refund of the purchase price!

Subtotal	
Sales Tax (AZ residents, 5%)	
S & H (10% of subtotal–min $4.00)	
Total (U.S. Funds only)	

CANADA: add 22% for S & H and G.S.T.

Method of payment (check one):
- ❏ Check or Money Order ❏ Visa
- ❏ MasterCard   ❏ Purchase Order Attached

Credit Card No. _____

Expires _____

Signature _____

Zephyr Press ®

REACHING THEIR HIGHEST POTENTIAL

To order write or call
P.O. Box 66006-W
Tucson, AZ 85728-6006
1-800-232-2187
FAX 520-323-9402
http://www.zephyrpress.com